ON
ISLAND
TIME

ON ISLAND TIME

Written and Illustrated by

HILARY STEWART

Douglas & McIntyre
Vancouver/Toronto

University of Washington Press
Seattle

Douglas & McIntyre Ltd.
2323 Quebec Street, Suite 201
Vancouver, British Columbia V5T 4S7

Canadian Cataloguing in Publication Data
Stewart, Hilary, 1924-
   On island time
   ISBN 1-55054-699-6
   1. Stewart, Hilary, 1924- 2. Quadra Island (B.C.)—Biography. 3. Natural history—British
Columbia—Quadra Island. I. Title.
FC3845.Q26Z49 1998   971.1'2   C98-910005-7
F1089.Q22S73 1998

Originated in Canada by Douglas & McIntyre and published simultaneously in the United States
of America by The University of Washington Press, PO Box 50096 Seattle, Washington 98145-5096

Library of Congress Cataloging-in-Publication Data
Stewart, Hilary
      On island time / written and illustrated by Hilary Stewart.
         p.   cm.
      ISBN 0-295-97830-9 (alk. paper)
      1. Quadra Island (B.C.)—Description and travel. 2. Natural history—British Columbia—
Quadra Island. 3. Stewart, Hilary—Homes and haunts—British Columbia—Quadra Island.
I. Title.
F1089.V3S78 1998   98-13060
917.11'2—dc21   CIP

Editing by Saeko Usukawa
Cover design by Val Speidel
Text design by DesignGeist
Cover photograph by Al Harvey

Printed and bound in Canada by Friesens
Printed on acid-free paper

The publisher gratefully acknowledges the support of the Canada Council for the Arts and of
the British Columbia Ministry of Tourism, Small Business and Culture. The publisher also
acknowledges the financial support of the Government of Canada through the Book Publishing
Industry Development Program for our publishing activities.

"Cry of the Wild Goose" words and music by Terry Gilkyson, ©1950 Warner/Chappell Music Co.
Inc. All rights reserved. Used by permission.

to Peter...

my brother
and buddy—

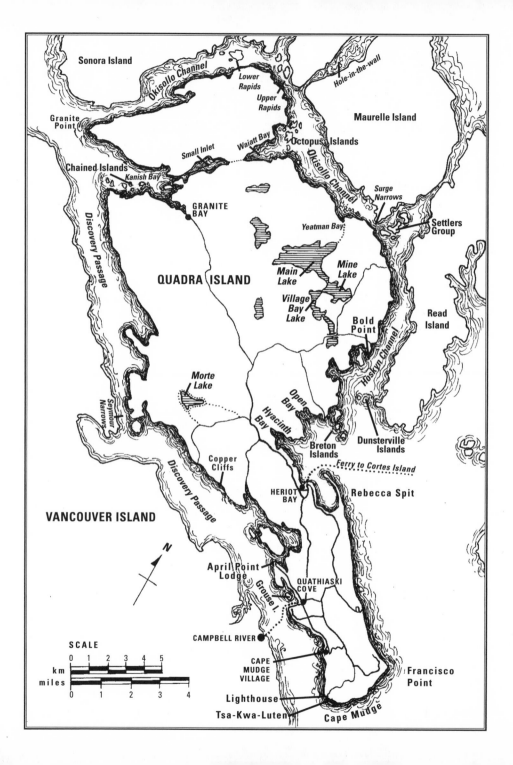

Contents

Acknowledgements

In writing about the various episodes, encounters and discoveries in this book, I sometimes needed to turn to

FAWN LILY

others for background information on island matters, as well as additional details and data. To those who readily gave of their time and knowledge to enrich the text and illustrations, or to assist in other ways, I extend my warm thanks: Wayne Assal, Sharon Brereton, Ted Davis, Joy Inglis, Judy Johnson, Heather Kellerhals-Stewart, Gilbert Krook, Nadine Mar, Don McEachern, Alana Mascali, Bruce Noble, Jeanette Taylor and Marcia Wolter.

I especially want to acknowledge the kind help, co-operation and enthuasiasm of biologist and naturalist Steve Mooney. His extensive knowledge of and interest in all that walks, crawls, flies, breathes, grows or thrives in the outdoors has been very helpful. And inspiring. Thank you, Steve.

A Wandering Foot

RUFUS-SIDED TOWHEE

I haven't quite figured out why islands are so special to me. Perhaps it is the element of the sea enclosing a defined space. Islands (small, of course, as they should be) allow for easy access to the sea—the sights, the sounds, the scents, and the rich life that abounds on, under and at the edge.

Perhaps my affinity for islands comes from being born on one—St. Lucia in the West Indies—as was my brother, Peter. My sister, Heather, was born on neighbouring St. Kitts. For us children, a tropical island was a bright and stimulating place to live and thrive. Best of all were the amber sand beaches and warm turquoise seas year round.

Eventually, when I was nine years old, our family returned to England. Boarding school was followed by four years in the Women's Auxiliary Air Force and then four years at St. Martin's School of Art in London.

An extraordinary coincidence involving Peter (who had meanwhile emigrated to Canada), changed the entire course of my life. I was nearing the end of my fourth year at art school, uncertain what I should do when I graduated. I was about to leave the house one morning when a letter arrived from Peter. The airmail stamp, I noticed, depicted a Canada goose in flight. And just then, the radio began playing a popular song of the time.

> My heart knows what the wild goose knows,
> And I must go where the wild goose goes.
> Wild goose, brother goose, which is best—
> A wandering foot or a heart at rest?

Right away, I knew what I must do: when I finished art school, I would choose the wandering foot and join my brother in Canada. I hurried to St. Martin's, threw open the door of my classroom, and declared: "I'm going to Canada!"

I was eager to live in an uncrowded land that boasted spectacular mountains, emerald lakes and endless forests of tall trees. I think that a year of living in Gwynymynydd, in the Welsh countryside, had done much to confirm the path and direction of my interest in the outdoors. I used to cycle many miles through valleys and over hills, walk stream edges, follow forest footpaths, always discovering, examining, collecting and sketching aspects of the natural world that ever lured me. One time, Peter (he was still living in Britain then) had cycled with me all the way to Hoylake, in Cheshire, where we had once lived, and back again. Our sister, Heather, was grown up and training to be a nurse in wartime Leicester, so she never had the chance to join in our escapades. But now we compensate for that by sharing interesting holidays in England and places like Santorini, the Scilly Isles, Morocco and Malta. And a return visit to St. Lucia.

I spent thirty-four wonderful and fulfilling years living and working in Vancouver, British Columbia, but always found the contrast between life in the city and time spent in sparsely populated areas to be profound. For me, the wilderness was like an underground stream that kept surfacing every now and again, briefly, refreshingly. Beckoning. I loved the city and much that it offered, yet my soul always knew that on any available weekend or holiday, it had to break out and take rural flight: to ranches, rivers and lakes in the Chilcotin, the Okanagan and the Kootenays; to the Fraser Canyon; and to coastal communities on Vancouver Island, the Gulf Islands, the San Juan Islands, the Queen Charlotte Islands. Islands.

   When eventually I came to settle on an island, I had a sense that I had come full circle, from St. Lucia in the West Indies to Quadra in the Discovery Islands, off the east coast of Vancouver Island which, in turn, is off the west coast of British Columbia. What a rich, wide circle it has been.

One day, my publisher, Scott McIntyre, suggested I write and illustrate a book about my being on Quadra Island. But with an active and enjoyable life in the community, I was reluctant to start another book. I consulted with Heather Kellerhals-Stewart (no relation), a much-published writer and friend who lives on Quadra. Her suggestion: "Make a list of headings—subjects you'd like to write about—and see if you get excited over it." Well . . . okay. That seemed a reasonable idea. A week later, I sat down and wrote:

   First visit to Quadra.
   Subsequent visits.
   Finding the property—weird!
   Meeting the owner—coincidence!
   Option to buy—another coincidence
   Procrastinating. Buying.
   Architects 1, 2, 3. Building. Problems.

Renting out the house.
Moving to Quadra, tackling the "jungle."

By this time, I found I was getting excited and kept going. I added headings which touched on encounters with deer, eagles, woodpeckers, a squirrel, bats, raccoons, windstorms, blow-downs, power outages, the wood stove, the witcher and the well, boulders, boats, ferries, petroglyphs—even mushrooms, mosses, lichens and insects. Whatever came my way, piqued my interest, brought delight or a new experience. Indecision receded like the outgoing tide.

I pulled out photos from my numerous albums, especially the ones full of flora and fauna taken over many years of travel throughout British Columbia, to use as a basis for my pen-and-ink illustrations. If I lacked certain species, I went out and made detailed sketches or photographed them. Any research material I needed was available on the island or in the nearby town of Campbell River, so different from flying to Ottawa, New York, Washington, Chicago, Alaska and other distant places which research for most of my other books on Northwest Coast First Nations cultures had required.

Since this book is not meant to be a documentation of Quadra Island and what it means to live here, I have chosen to keep the contents mainly personal and largely close to home, focussing on the natural world rather than on social and cultural events.

There are many islands off the coast of British Columbia, some near, some remote; some easily accessible, some not; some heavily populated, some with but a scattering of hardy souls. Islands are not for everyone, especially when you miss that last ferry home and have to try to find a vacancy in a motel or hotel at the height of the tourist season—or sleep in your car till morning and the next ferry.

Chapter 1

Taking Rural Flight

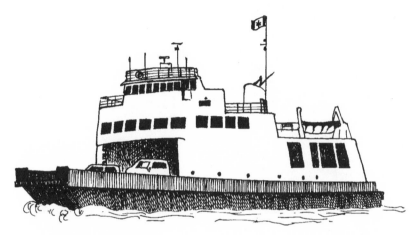

"QUADRA QUEEN II"

T he small ferry crosses Discovery Passage, swings around a high rocky point into the calm water of a cove, slows, and gently comes nose to nose with the dock. To the left, two big net lofts on stilts jostle for waterfront space with a cannery, sheds, houses, jetties and wharfs. A forested hill rises behind.

From the city of Vancouver, Bill and I have taken the big ferry from Horseshoe Bay to Nanaimo, on Vancouver Island, and driven two-and-a-half

"CORTES QUEEN"

BALD EAGLE TAKING DEAD FISH

hours up island to the town of Campbell River, to board this small ferry to Quadra Island.

As we drive off the ferry and along the red-railed dock, Bill says to me, "This is Quathiaski Cove." I think to myself: "I'm never going to remember that name." "It's pretty," I say.

We drive across Quadra Island, which is heavily treed, to another bay and another dock, then board an even smaller ferry to go to Cortes Island, where Bill has a summer cottage on a lake (and a canoe). As the ferry pulls out, we get out of the car and lean over the ship's rail. Heriot Bay sparkles with small bright boats tied up at the floating wharfs; those at anchor do a tottering dance to the ferry's wash as it moves out and swings around. Someone on shore is tossing out fish heads or something, and Bald Eagles begin flying in to enjoy an easy feast. First two, then three, then five eagles and more swirl around, landing, screeching, grabbing, and taking off again in a tumble of black and white.

The ferry slides past the end of a long spit, sending scoters and Buffleheads skittering out of its way. "That's Rebecca Spit," Bill points out. Such is my first, though brief, introduction to Quadra Island.

The second time that Bill and I head for his cottage, we miss the last ferry to Cortes and stay on Quadra Island at the Heriot Bay Inn, a large white historic wooden building overlooking the bay, with islands and moun-

HERIOT BAY INN

tains beyond. Another time en route to Cortes, we stop to camp near Heriot Bay at Rebecca Spit, a narrow strip of forested land curving along the east side of Drew Harbour. Like a long protective arm, the spit shelters a flock of assorted watercraft from easterly winds. Bill and I scramble over drift logs and walk the beach. A full moon hauls itself up from behind the mainland Coast Mountains, laying down a bright path over the now ambered sea, reaching all the way to our feet at tide's edge. A loon calls out with that eerie, quavering sound which, for some reason, is always so special. I like this island, and by now I have learned to pronounce Quathiaski Cove.

A few years later, my good friend and colleague, anthropologist Joy Inglis, takes early retirement. She and her husband, Bob, leave Vancouver to make their home on some waterfront property—on Quadra Island. Not long after that, I move into a house on Point Grey Road, in Vancouver, that is owned by Rolf and Heather Kellerhals, who happen to live on Quadra Island. Coincidence?

COMMON LOON

JOY AND BOB INGLIS' BEACH CABIN

From time to time, I take the ferry to Vancouver Island and drive north to Campbell River, then head to Strathcona Park Lodge Outdoor Education Centre to spend a week or so as a resource person for its courses on Survival in the Wilderness or Native Indian Lifestyle, encamped on the outer west coast of Vancouver Island. On the way home, I frequently make a side trip to Cortes Island if Bill is there, or visit Joy and Bob on Quadra. They have a guest cabin built on the edge of the beach; the windows face eastward, out to the Coast Mountains and some islands I can't name, although I know one is Cortes. Eagles frequent the beach and perch on the tall conifers. Herons stalk the tide pools. Somewhere far off to the south is the city of Vancouver, and I feel a twinge of reluctance to return there.

One spring, I spend a week on Cortes with Bill, followed by a visit with Joy and Bob on Quadra. After lunch, I drive to Quathiaski Cove to catch the 2 P.M. ferry, looking forward to spending time at Strathcona Park Lodge. Suddenly, my car swings left into a private driveway, where a small sign says FOR SALE. I think, "What's this? I'm going for the ferry— what's going on here?" The driveway splits into two, and I take the right-hand fork, which curves around a stand of tall trees.

. . . MY CAR SWINGS LEFT INTO A PRIVATE DRIVEWAY . . .

The car comes to a stop in front of a monster, cream-coloured mobile home. I find myself opening the car door and approaching the trailer; its 18.3-m (64-foot) length seems to go on forever. A woman comes out to the door and looks at me expectantly. I remember the sign. "Is this for sale?" I blurt out rather stupidly.

"Yes," she says.

What do I say next? "How many acres?" I ask.

"Three, and the trailer is included, and it has an addition at the back." She tells me the children are growing up and the family really needs to move to a bigger place . . .

GREAT BLUE HERON

9

I look around. The trailer sits in a large grassy meadow that is dotted with single mature trees and surrounded by forest. "We have horses," she explains, "so when we cleared the land, we left some shade trees for them." She invites me in. There is bright red shag carpet throughout. When I ask the price, she says, "Well, you really ought to talk to my husband, but he is at work right now. He works on the ferry."

"That's just where I'm headed," I tell her.

"Ask for Jack McTavish," she says. I thank her and return to my car.

As I board the 3 P.M. ferry, I ponder: what made me turn left like that? I realize that at the back of my mind I have been thinking perhaps I should have a place of my own, but I am always too busy to do anything about it.

On the ferry, I ask for Jack McTavish and am directed upstairs to the wheelhouse. We talk about the property, but within ten minutes the ferry is arriving in Campbell River. "Look," says Jack, "if you aren't in a hurry, just stay on board and we'll talk some more." On the journey back to Quathiaski Cove, he introduces me to the purser, who just happens to be a real estate agent. The purser opens a drawer and pulls out a pad of option-to-buy forms, explaining that an option to buy carries no obligation; but should someone else wish to purchase the land, I get first chance. I can always change my mind. More discussion, and now the ferry is heading back to the other side again.

All this shuttling back and forth ends when I write a cheque for $1,000.00—which of course I don't have in my account—and ask him not to cash it for four days. I drive to Strathcona Park Lodge, thinking, "What have I done? Three acres? A 60-foot trailer? Red shag carpet? Well . . . I can always back out." When I arrive at the lodge, I throw open the door and triumphantly announce: "I've just bought property on Quadra Island!"

Once back in Vancouver, however, I am caught up in curating an exhibition on early Northwest Coast aboriginal fishing methods, promoting the book I have written and illustrated on that subject, and giving a lot of lectures on archaeology, artifacts and fishing technologies. Also, I am a resource person on a river-rafting trip and an educational cruise to Alaska. And I fly to Turkey for three weeks: Dr. James Russell of the Department of

Classics at the University of British Columbia has asked me to make drawings of artifacts from a major archaeological dig at Anamurium.

If I give a thought to that property on Quadra Island, I quickly dismiss it: no time. That is, until I get a phone call from Jack McTavish. He is really anxious to sell the property and drops the price. Something in my head says BUY IT. So I do. The first year, I rent the trailer to the Royal Canadian Mounted Police for an office and to various others who come and go. In long hot summers when the well runs dry, I have to pay for truckloads of water for my tenants. Or I have the roof fixed, or the stove repaired, or the septic tank pumped out.

On a summer day in 1979, I travel up to Quadra for a notable occasion, the opening of the Kwagiulth Museum in Cape Mudge. The village of Cape Mudge, south of Quathiaski Cove, is generally referred to as "the Village" by islanders. It is home to about four hundred members of the We-Wai-Kai band of the Kwagiulth First Nations people. In addition to rows of well-kept homes, the village has the new museum, its own dock, fire department, community hall, swimming pool, tennis court and playground. It also has a historic mission church and belltower, built in 1931.

Fifty-seven years ago, many masks and other ceremonial regalia were confiscated by the Canadian government when officials raided a Kwagiulth potlatch on upcoast Village Island. Without understanding the true nature of the potlatch, the government had outlawed the ceremony, which was a key part of Native life. The law was finally rescinded in 1952. After lengthy negotiations which have gone on for many years, the government is finally returning these treasures to the people of Cape Mudge. An attractive museum has been built to house the potlatch collection. Much tradition and ceremony surround this momentous occasion, as people rejoice and celebrate having their family heirlooms back where they belong. Along with speeches, dancing in ceremonial button blankets and drumming, feasting plays a major part. The sumptuous sit-down meal in the community hall requires 682 kg (1,500 pounds) of fire-roasted salmon to feed the crowd.

Finally, after researching and writing a book about Haida artist Robert

Davidson's prints, I take the time to think about putting a house on my property and approach an architect friend, Judah Shumiatcher. We go up to Quadra and visit the property. Some weeks later, he presents me with a set of plans, and I make a complete scale model of the house. It is quite gorgeous, with multiangular rooms, interesting roof lines and a sunken living room. But I realize it is too large and too expensive to build. Judah modifies the plans, but it is still not "island." I am not at all sure what an "island house" should look like, but I am sure that I will know it when I see it.

Then I become very involved researching and writing a book called *Looking at Indian Art of the Northwest Coast* and forget about the house, until I run into an old friend, Charles Laubental, a retired architect. I tell him about my property and problems. "I'd love to design a house for you," he says, "it will give me something to do." I tell him I just want a small house for my retirement, nothing elaborate. A few weeks later, I receive the plans. It seems to be a nice house, compact and convenient; it even includes a small walled garden. So I make a complete scale model of it, and then realize it is an ideal and charming little house for retirement—in the suburbs. It's just not "island" either.

My interest in botany and wilderness survival leads to writing a book on wild teas, coffees and cordials. In the fall, I make a special trip to Strathcona Park Lodge to attend their first Folk Weekend of music and crafts, now an annual event. When I am about to leave, in comes Rob Wood, an experienced outdoorsman who lives on Maurelle Island just east of Quadra and who has designed some of the rustic chalets and buildings at the lodge. As we talk, the subject of my house-design problem comes up. Being an island person, Rob is empathetic and asks what I want in a house. Briefly, I list my architectural requirements, but just as important, I describe how it should look and feel. The house should be simple, earthy, airy and interesting; the space should flow, and I want a lot of wood, lots of windows and decking. Rob understands. "Tell you what I'll do," he says. "I'll go see the lot, make some preliminary drawings, and send them to you. If you like them, we'll go ahead. And if you don't, that's okay."

In the meantime, I'm off to the Field Museum in Chicago to write all the

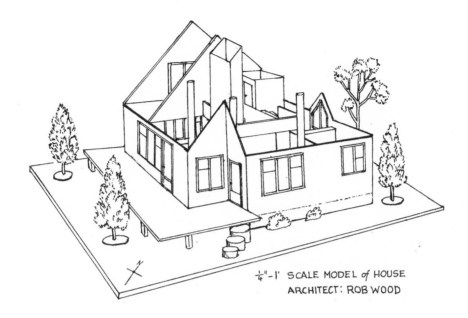

$\frac{1}{4}$"-1' SCALE MODEL of HOUSE
ARCHITECT: ROB WOOD

labelling for a permanent exhibition entitled "Maritime Peoples of the Northwest Coast." I also continue to give lectures at schools, museums, colleges and universities. So busy am I with work that I almost forget about the idea of a house for my property, until a large manila envelope slides through my mail slot and plops onto the hall floor. It's a set of architectural drawings from Rob Wood. The first sheet is a drawing of the house elevation. "That's it!" I say aloud. Excited, I unfold the plans: log posts rising up from the ground floor and log beams supporting the joists for the cathedral ceiling. Skylights. An upper storey for a studio or guest room, with a half bathroom, plus a small open area that looks down onto the living room below. Decking that wraps around three sides. Lots of windows—though I want them nearly to the floor, and there are too many of them, leaving not enough wall space for bookshelves and artworks.

From the plans, I make yet a third scale model that includes the minimal

JULY. 1982

changes I want. The model's roof lifts off to expose the upper floor, and the upper floor lifts out to reveal the ground floor: chimney stack and raised hearth for a wood stove, living and dining room areas, kitchen, hall, bedroom and bathroom. In all, just 112 m² (1200 square feet). With the changes, it's perfect.

Rob suggests hiring Bob Harris and Larry Hansen, island builders with a feel for wooden houses: cedar walls, spruce ceilings, log posts and beams. From time to time, I make a quick trip up to Quadra to check on progress, discuss some design aspects or solve unexpected problems. On an early visit, I find the posts and beams in place, and the joists and 2 x 4 framing of the outside wall complete. But I notice that the openings for the windows are all for traditional sizes, with sills about thigh height. The original plans showed this, but I had asked the builders for tall windows with a low sill height for more light and a better view of the outdoors. All the double-glazed windows are already on site and the builders are reluctant to return them and order

1 4

new ones. But I am adamant, even though I know it means an extra expense for me. Happily, they agree to make the change, recognizing its advantages. More than just builders, Bob and Larry are skilled, caring craftsmen with heart and a sense of aesthetics.

I climb up a ladder to look at the second floor where the peaked roof will form the ceiling, and have an idea. The blueprints call for a pony wall at each end of the room, with storage behind. A pony wall is a low wall, in this case 1.5 m (5 feet) from the floor to the sloping ceiling. I can see that by eliminating the pony wall on one side (I won't need the extra storage), the skylight can be repositioned lower down the roof to offer a vista of trees in addition to sky. I ask the builders if that can be done. Yes it can.

On other visits, I continue to discuss aspects of design and solve small problems, as well as deciding where to place lighting fixtures and electrical outlets. I draw up plans for the layout of kitchen and bathrooms and meet with a cabinetmaker to discuss how I want the cupboards to look. Sometimes I bring items like ceramic tiles, recessed teak pulls for drawers and cupboards, or sculptured ash door handles and lighting fixtures. One time, my helpful brother hauls up some purchases like folding louvred closet doors and a front door inset with a stained-glass window representing a rising sun. His equally helpful wife, Anne, works to clear away young alders from around the house. They sleep in sleeping bags on the kitchen floor and I on the bathroom floor, the only clean areas in the half-built house. We cook breakfast on a primus stove in the carport.

Back in Vancouver, I choose countertop materials, the bathtub, the toilets, the washbasins and all the taps. I find a beautiful cast-iron wood stove and have it shipped up. The roof shakes are hand split on the island. I choose carpeting from a Campbell River flooring company.

One of these visits to Quadra is for quite a different and exciting purpose. Joy phones to tell me that during an extremely low tide, a ferry crew member noticed a long row of multiple wooden stumps sticking out of the beach gravel and stones on the Campbell River side. These are short and mostly around 7 cm (3 inches) in diameter. Joy thinks they are likely the remains of an ancient fish trap, uncovered due to winter storms. Would I be

WOODEN STAKES OF FISH TRAP

interested in looking at it? Since I'd published a book on early Northwest Coast Native fishing methods, I am indeed interested, and head up to Campbell River right away. Racing against an incoming tide, Joy and I plot the positions of hundreds of the stakes, which end with a stone alignment. I file the results with the (then) British Columbia Provincial Museum.

Finally, in August 1982, my house is finished, but I can't move in because I still need the amenities and resources of the city for my work. I phone a rental agency in Campbell River for house tenants, with the result that the owner of the agency moves in with his family, and they stay for three years. A string of other tenants follow—good and bad.

For eight years, I keep the scale model of my house on a shelf so I can look at it; I even landscape it with twigs and hardhack seed heads. Now and again, I take off the roof, remove the upper floor, and walk my fingers through the ground floor, imagining myself living there. I cut pieces of art card to represent my furnishings and plan where each piece will go. I want so much to live in this house, perfect for me in every way, designed around my needs and desires. But every year it seems just out of reach. There is always another book to research, write and illustrate.

My next book, *Cedar: Tree of Life to the Northwest Coast Indians*, takes four years of intense but deeply fascinating research. In between working on my own books, there are requests to illustrate others, such as *Wisdom of the Elders* by Ruth Kirk and *Gathering What the Great Nature Provided* by the Native elders of 'Ksan.

Joy Inglis, who has studied Kwagiulth culture for over thirty years, asks if I will do some photography, maps and illustrations for a book she is working on with Harry Assu, hereditary chief of Cape Mudge. (The book, titled *Assu of Cape Mudge* is published later, in 1989.) The chief and his family are friends of Joy's, and he spends countless hours with her and her tape recorder, relaying not only his history but telling of early events which incorporate legendary and mythical creatures (a reminder here that the word myth is defined as an ancient story handed down from the past).

Instead of simply listening to the tape recordings I am to illustrate, Joy invites me up to Quadra to meet Chief Assu and to visit the places where the events took place. The first is in Gowlland Harbour, only accessible by boat, so Harry takes us in his 16-foot runabout. Standing on the beach, he looks out over the harbour and recalls an event that took place here. It pertains to the skin of a blue whale, rigged to carry four men inside, being towed back and forth across to Stag Island, and how the men perished. I make reference sketches and notes of the harbour, Stag Island and the vista beyond, asking him questions to help me visualize the entire scene. Since Harry Assu is a descendant of the People of the Whale House and the Whale is one of his crests, his memory of the dramatic episode is still vivid.

Later, the three of us take the ferry across to Campbell River and drive to the spit where the Cape Mudge people lived before moving to Quadra. We sit together on a log on the beach, at the place where Harry says his father once lay sick in a tent shelter; being close to the water was considered healthy and would hasten recovery. In the night, a large pod of whales beached themselves on the pebbly shore. One of them told the ailing man to cook and eat the headless salmon that would come to the water's edge.

1 7

THE CHAMBER-POT ROCK

The whales, Harry explains, were sharing their food with his father, who did as he was instructed and soon became well. Again, I make sketches of the background of the scene, with Quadra in the distance. There is a tall pole just behind where we are sitting; I happen to look up, and there, perched on the top, is a large mature eagle looking, not out to sea but down—at us.

On the return ferry to Quadra, just as we are entering Quathiaski Cove, Joy and Harry point out another feature I am to draw. It is a large, bulging formation in the bedrock, with a deep hollow that forms a bowl with a distinctive rim. Harry says that to his Kwakwala-speaking people, the name of the cove, Quathiaski, sounds like their word for pisspot. It's very apt, but I can't help feeling relieved that I don't have to tell people that I own property in Pisspot Cove.

In 1984, another good excuse for me to leave the city and head up to Quadra is an invitation from Joy and Bob to spend the weekend to attend and take part in a very special event. After the people of Cape Mudge renovated their heritage church and opened it to everyone on the island, they commissioned the noted Haida artist Bill Reid to create a carved motif for the reredos wall behind the altar. He visited the church, sat there and meditated, then decided on a design of two circling salmon, male and female. He, together with Haida carver Jim Hart, produced a masterpiece on yellow cedar boards.

This is a fitting theme, as many of the Cape Mudge residents are fishermen, as were countless generations before them, and salmon is the most important fish to them. As part of the dedication of the newly installed carving, Cape Mudge plans to observe the First Salmon Ceremony, an event once held along almost all the Northwest Coast. It took various forms in different areas, but always the focus was on respecting the salmon and welcoming its annual return. The subject is near to my heart because I researched and wrote about this ceremony in my book on aboriginal fishing, and am happy to be invited to speak about it on this occasion. This ceremony will be different because times have changed, but the essence will be similar.

A newly made cedar bark mat is an essential part of the proceedings, and Joy, together with some women in the village, takes on this task. They pull the bark from a cedar tree, dry and split it, then weave the strands into a large mat, working in the lower hall of the Kwagiulth Museum. Several other women are there on another project, sewing button blankets for an upcoming potlatch to be given by Chief Harry Assu. He is following the custom of giving a potlatch one year after the death of a spouse.

On the day of the First Salmon Ceremony, Joy, Bob and I go to the village, and there, against a background of sea and snow-capped mountains, are four (a spiritual number) large salmon roasting by a fire, tended by an elder.

QUADRA ISLAND UNITED CHURCH

FIRST SALMON CEREMONY

The first part of the ceremony is held in the church, whose altar is covered in a specially made button blanket depicting the Tree of Life. The minister, the Rev. Ronald Atkinson, is wearing a button blanket (given to him by the congregation) which he reserves for special occasions. Bill Reid is not able to attend the dedication of his carving because he is in Paris, but Jim Hart is there to see the splendour of their work in place. The fragrance from the large cedar boughs placed along the base of the wall and the sunlight warming the leaping salmon carved on the yellow cedar combine to create a powerful and moving scene. I feel honoured to be part of the service, part of a ceremony which is being revived after lying dormant for the past seventy years.

When the service is over, everyone walks over to the beach where a table displays the four fire-roasted salmon on the new cedar bark mat. Filing past, we all help ourselves to a piece of succulent fish. Finally, according to tradition, the bones and all the inedible parts of the salmon are wrapped up in the mat, together with some stones, and carried to the water's edge where the crowd gathers. The scene is awash with the beautiful red and blue button blankets worn by Kwagiulth men and women, the white buttons outlining their family crests gleaming in the afternoon sun.

A herring skiff arrives, carrying, in the bow, twin sisters Mabel and Emma Sewid. In early times, twins were believed to have been salmon before birth and thus to have a special rapport with them. The cedar bundle is handed to the sisters, and, as the skiff leaves, Bobby Joseph, who has been drumming at the water's edge, says a farewell in the Kwakwala language. The twins place the salmon remains in the ocean, an ancient gesture that enables the fish to become whole again and return to their village at the far edge of the sea, the horizon. They will tell the Salmon People that they were treated with respect by the humans, so now all the other salmon will swim across the ocean and go on up the rivers, presenting themselves to provide food for the people.

Long, long ago, First Nations people recognized that to respect the salmon was to ensure its return in abundance every year. I think about this most timely and appropriate lesson. Since the salmon are in decline all along the coast, it must be due to a long-term lack of respect, such as the destruction and alteration of their habitat.

After the publication of *The Adventures and Sufferings of John R. Jewitt, Captive of Maquinna,* I do research for a book on totem poles, which calls for a lot of travel from the British Columbia border to Alaska. Then I decide it is finally time to make the move to my Quadra house. In preparation, because of the eight years of wear and tear and abuse on the original carpeting, I have the whole house recarpeted in an off-white Berber.

On moving day, a huge truck arrives at my Vancouver home and loads almost everything. My brother, Peter, comes from his home in the Okanagan, bringing a small van to haul the well-packed, fragile items to ensure their safety.

This is it. Peter is at the curb, the van loaded, engine running. I am carrying my purse, the vacuum cleaner and the model of the Quadra house. As

I pull the front door shut behind me, the model slips from my fingers and falls to the porch floor. The brittle glue of years lets go, and the model shatters into dozens of pieces. My immediate distress is quickly replaced by the symbolism this represents: I no longer need this cardboard mockup because I am on my way to the real thing. I gather up the fragments, drop them into the garbage can, and climb into the van beside Peter. We're off. I am leaving behind thirty-four years of city living. I am going to my very own house—on an island.

C h a p t e r   2

Becoming an Islander

Although it is February, there is still snow on the Vancouver Island highway, and it gets deeper as Peter and I head north for Quadra. It has snowed heavily there, too, and Bob Inglis tries to get a snowplough to clear my driveway for our arrival, but none is available. Eventually, he bribes someone to come by offering one of his famous cheesecakes. Bob also organizes helpers to unload the moving van, which gets there shortly before Peter and I do. The huge van has trouble manoeuvring the curved driveway, and the marks made by one wheel sliding into the ditch remain visible for years to come. Bob divides the helpers into "outies" and "innies." The former unload everything from the van and take it to the door; the latter carry it all inside the house while I direct what goes where. This prevents snow from being tramped indoors onto the new carpeting.

At last, I am in my own house. Designed for me. Built for me. I have spent eight years watching other people living in it, waiting for this time when it would be mine completely. Within twenty-four hours, I feel entirely at home, both in the house and on the island.

Peter stays a few days to help me get set up, working enthusiastically on over twenty things that need doing to get me settled: moving furniture, hanging paintings, adding shelving and much more. He is just marvellous; I could not have made the move without his help. After he leaves, it still takes several weeks for me to fix up all the scuffs, scratches, dents, nail holes and breaks around the house, a legacy of various tenants, and, as I will hear later, some memorable parties.

The house's appearance is marred by a many-fingered TV antenna atop a tall skinny pole that is lashed to the balcony of the room upstairs. Since I don't have a TV set, I undo the lashing and give the pole a push. It falls with a thunk; two of the metallic fingers dig into the earth and are bent. The aged antenna doesn't seem to be in good enough shape to sell, and it won't burn or compost. So I take it down to the roadside and leave it there with a sign that says, "If you can use this—have it." The next day it is gone.

In spite of making many friends and beginning to feel comfortable on the island, I know I am still a newcomer in several ways. One day in April, not long after I've moved to Quadra, a friend on the island, Babs Brereton, phones me. "A couple of us are going swimming in the river," she says. "Would you like to join us?"

"The river?" I say in disbelief. "You're crazy, it's much too cold for swimming."

"No," she replies, "it'll be warm."

"Swimming in the river warm? You must be insane."

"No," Babs insists, "it's heated."

"What's heated?" I ask.

"The pool," she replies.

"A heated pool in the river?" This seems to me quite extraordinary.

"Yes," Babs says.

"What 'pool' are you talking about?"

"The swimming pool at Strathcona Gardens over in Campbell River," she says.

Then I understand. I'm still so new to Quadra that I don't know that islanders refer to the town across the water as "the River." In turn, the inhabitants there refer to Quadra Island as "the Rock."

I also learn that when you give your phone number to another islander, you omit the first three numbers—because they're the same for everybody. When I see a notice informing islanders that the library has moved to larger premises "in the old Credit Union building," I am puzzled because I have no idea where the Credit Union used to be. Similarly, a poster advertising an event at the island Community Centre ends with "tickets from the usual outlets," and I have to ask what those are. Quite often, the answer to a question such as "Where does he live?" is "In the old Walker place," or "Next to the old Jones farm." It's as though the previous owners serve as a signpost or give a historical permanence to the property, a spoken memorial to an old-timer. I wonder if, should I live here long enough, my place will someday be known as "the old Hilary house."

I often check my watch by the single toot that the ferry gives one minute before leaving Quathiaski Cove, as the signal is audible from my place. I've figured out that if you are a foot passenger and have just parked your car, you should begin to hurry when you hear the warning. It takes one minute at least to walk the long dock.

In the lounge on the ferry, there is usually a sprinkling of people that I know, and we spend the twelve-minute crossing catching up on news, discussing gardening or reading the cluttered notice board. Small children rattle loose around the fore and aft lounges, crawling under the rows of seats in exciting games. On some trips, a large cardboard box is set out, filled with a jumble of children's clothing; the thick felt-penned words on the box say it all: LOST AND FOUND.

The first ferry service to make more or less regular crossings started in 1949. The privately owned 38-foot *Victory II* carried twelve passengers and ran on diesel fuel and a provincial government subsidy. Ten years later, she was replaced by the 70-foot *Uchuk*, which could carry up to a hundred passengers—but no cars. It was another ten years before the islanders got a car ferry. Built for the run and proudly named the *Quadra Queen I*, she carried 16 cars and 129 passengers. The ensuing years brought larger and more sophisticated vessels as Quadra's population increased.

Islanders have a love/hate relationship with their ferry that depends on the time of day or year, the number of logging trucks using it, the overloads in tourist season and the time of the last sailing (that may not allow you to see the end of a lengthy movie or theatre performance in "the River"). Plus, there is the inconvenience of dangerous cargo runs when no passengers are allowed, and of course the vagaries of weather. The local paper, published every two weeks, carries a cartoon pertinent to island issues; from time to time, one pokes fun at some aspect of the ferry, and these get pinned up in the crew lounge.

I haven't been living for long on Quadra when I have an odd experience with the ferry on the way back from "the River," where I'd gone to pick up office and art supplies not available on Quadra. The sunshine is gleaming on the snow on the ridge of mountains which form a background to Campbell River, so I take a window seat in the stern lounge to enjoy the sight. As the ferry heads back to Quathiaski Cove, the city diminishes, sliding into the distance.

After a while, I notice that we are heading northwest, going up Discovery Passage, instead of crossing it. In fact, the ferry is now well past its destination of Quathiaski Cove. That's odd. I look around the lounge, but I don't happen to know any of the few passengers who are either chatting, reading, resting with closed eyes or simply not looking out the window. Nobody else has noticed anything unusual, so I sit and wait. The boat continues heading up Discovery Passage, past Campbell River Spit and Painters Lodge, then past April Point Lodge on Quadra Island.

Where are we going? There is no announcement, nothing. Have we been hijacked? After a few more minutes of continued northwesterly sailing, my curiosity becomes tinged with concern. I decide to go up to the wheelhouse and find out what's going on. I climb the narrow stairs marked in large letters CREW ONLY, come to a door, and open it. There is *no one there*, and I experience a moment of panic. On a table in a small room to the left are coffee cups, sugar and cream, a folded newspaper, a packet of cigarettes, an ashtray and a book. Raingear hangs on pegs in a neat row nearby. This is not just weird, it's spooky . . . like the *Marie Celeste* ghost ship. I notice a closed door ahead and carefully turn the knob to open it. There, in the wheelhouse, are two men, one at the helm. It gives me a measure of comfort to see that they are wearing B.C. Ferry uniforms.

"Ah . . . excuse me," I say trying to sound casual and at ease, "would you mind telling me just where it is we are headed? I had thought . . ."

"Oh," says the captain, interrupting, "we're just testing a new engine—we'll be heading back shortly." Just testing. I return to my window seat somewhat bemused but reassured. I should have known that nobody would ever hijack Quadra's little ferry.

On other occasions while crossing Discovery Passage by ferry, I become aware of a shift in the ship's direction and look out to see a huge freighter sliding by, or a tug hauling a couple of barges loaded with freight. In summer, the passing vessel may be a sleek and imposing cruise ship returning from Alaska on its way to Vancouver or Seattle. One calm night, returning home from a show, ferry passengers are treated to the site of two massive cruise ships, every deck lit up from bow to stern, sailing past each other. The placid waters reflect the spectacle of lights into a brilliant double image gliding through the ebony night.

From one end to the other, Quadra Island measures 37 km (23 miles) as the eagle flies. Its wide northern end, rising up in rocky bluffs and mountainous peaks, is short on roads and population, but to make up for that it has a scattering of lovely lakes and a sprawl of hiking trails. Some areas here still are old growth, but almost all of the island's forests are second growth dating from the late nineteenth to the early twentieth century. As yet the island is still largely forested, but clearcut logging marches on—sometimes too close for comfort.

The island's contours seem to have been largely cut out with a fretsaw, creating an abundance of bays, coves, harbours and headlands along its ragged coast, with the leftover bits flung aside to form offshore islands. Closely hugging its northern and eastern coast are Sonora, Maurelle and Read—all, along with Quadra itself, part of the Discovery Islands off the east coast of Vancouver Island. Beaches are few—mostly pebbly—and all of them surrender to a full moon's high tide.

Southward, the broad bulk of Quadra slims down considerably. The village of Heriot Bay is clustered around a heritage hotel, docks, wharfs, stores, a post office and houses. Rural roads meander their way between Heriot Bay and Quathiaski Cove, sprouting occasional side roads. Long driveways heading off into forested properties indicate a larger population than in the north.

Quathiaski Cove, generally referred to as "the Cove," also has stores, a post office, docks, wharfs, a lot of fishboats, a pub and a sprinkling of houses among trees.

The southernmost end of the island terminates in a high sandy bluff. Wide expanses of rock and boulder-strewn beaches, bare at low tide, wrap around the cape named for Zachary Mudge, a ship's officer who came ashore there in 1792 with explorer Captain George Vancouver.

Now that I've settled into the house, it's time to turn my attention to the property. I watch where the sun travels through the day, making note of which trees block the morning sun, which trees provide shade at noon, which let the afternoon sun through. First, I decide to tackle the driveway. All the tenants who'd lived in the house had used only the left side of the circular drive because it is a little shorter than the right side, so the unused half of the circle is wildly overgrown with broom, young alders, salmonberry and salal. One area has hemlock branches sweeping across the drive. I decide to restore the circle and spend many, many hours cutting off, pulling up, digging out and hauling away. Then I drag in bags of gravel from a beach and fill in the hollows.

SWORD FERN

From the dark of the forest beyond, I dig out clumps of stunted, short-of-light sword ferns and transplant them to each side of the driveway. One day, I visit friends Ray and Joyce who, it happens, have just dug out thirty or more sword ferns from their property and don't want them. I load this welcome treasure into my hatch-back, soil spilling all over, and bring them home to add to the driveway. The next week, I pass a piece of land that is being cleared. Huge, dug-up ferns edge the ditch by the road. "You keeping those ferns?" I ask a man nearby. "Help yourself," he says, but when I try to lift them, they are too heavy. The man helpfully takes over and another six ferns hit the hatch-back. Now I have over a hundred swashbuckling sword ferns, but I still need more.

DEER TRAIL

The drive encircles a large stand of conifers, two alders, a wild cherry and a stately, multiple-trunked Broad-leafed Maple; a wide and ancient deer trail cuts right through it like a freeway. I have to presume it is old because the trail itself is like a trough in the forest floor. As I explore more of the woods around the property, I discover several wide, well-worn deer trails that link up—or would do if a meadow had not been created by the previous owners for their horses. I notice that the deer cross the high-grass meadow along a regular route that meanders around the humps and hollows of the land's contours, until it reaches the forest cover again. In the forest, the deer have a network of narrow trails branching off the "freeways," heading this way and that, as though they had short attention spans. For no obvious reason, deer will stop using a particular trail through the underbrush, and it soon becomes overgrown again. But if I take clippers and open up the trail, they return to using it. Their freeways, however, are always wide and clear.

I am fascinated and charmed by these elegant animals that are living, moving garden ornaments, either passing through or staying to browse for an hour. Whatever I am doing, I stop to watch them, sometimes for twenty minutes. At first, whenever I went out onto the deck, they would gradually drift away to continue grazing at a little distance. Or, heads up, they would stand immobile, just staring at me. But over time, they have come to realize that I offer no threat; they lift their heads at my presence, then give a tail flick and return their attention to the grass.

Spring turns wonderfully warm with a good spell of no rain. But the fine weather means that I must minimize my use of water to ensure the well won't run dry, as it has in the past for my tenants. To cut back on the water flow, I take short showers and do some of the laundry by hand, when possible, to avoid the copious amounts of water the washer uses. Bowls of hair rinse and other grey water I save

BUCK BROWSING

and carry out to water the plants in tubs and the flower bed.

My well is a what is known as a "dug well" or "shallow well." It is near the driveway, down by the road, and is capped by a heavy cement lid. With a 2 x 4, I pry up the lid to take a peek. My face is reflected in the water's surface some distance below. I don't even know how deep the well is. A few feet away is a small shed housing the electric pump which sends the water uphill to the house. Having lived in a major city for over thirty years, I realize I don't know a whole lot about things like wells, and remind myself to go to the little local library (I now know where it is) to find out more.

While walking back to the house, I hear an odd and unfamiliar scratching sound. I turn to see a fat furry raccoon scrambling up the trunk of a hemlock tree. I had always thought they were nocturnal. The creature reaches a long branch off to one side, about 9 m (30 feet) up, makes a left turn onto it, and disappears behind the foliage. Almost immediately, there is the yowling, screeching sound of a fracas, and down from the branch plummets one raccoon.

THE RACCOON LOOKS UP...

The moment it hits the ground, the vanquished creature takes off running at full speed—heading directly towards me. I am frozen in fascination and watch wide-eyed, until I realize that the distance between us is diminishing fast. I have to do something quickly, so I clap my hands and shout. The raccoon looks up and, anxious not to face another enemy so soon, makes a swift right-angled turn and vanishes into the forest. I am left wondering what that was all about and how the raccoon could fall from such a height and not get hurt.

LUPIN

On the way back up to the house, I notice a small cluster of young, wild lupin leaves in the meadow, edging the drive and across a bank that slopes up toward the forest. I recall driving up from Vancouver to Quadra some years earlier and passing a steep, sloping cutbank awash in periwinkle blue. The tall spikes of the wild lupin formed a striking blur along the highway and I knew that I had to have some for my property. Heading up island again that fall, I stopped and scrambled up the bank to gather a handful of the crispy, charcoal-grey seed pods. On Quadra, I flung the seeds into the long grass of my meadow, where they flourished over the years.

Now here they are again, the young spring leaves bursting their way through

OX-EYED DAISY

the tangle of winter weary grasses. I look forward to the blue spires, especially now that they won't be in a blur.

When I survey the meadow, areas of it seem wide open, mostly grass, except for two enormous bushes of yellow broom, colourful but not really satisfying. I have always enjoyed the sight of fields extravagant with tall white Ox-Eyed Daisies, yellow centred, waving in a warm summer wind. So I dig up large quantities of these daisies from roadsides and transplant them in my meadow, where they thrive in the poor soil and hot sun.

A longtime friend and avid environmentalist, Melda Buchanan of Comox, on Vancouver Island, comes to visit me, bringing a gift of a swallow nesting box which she has made. I am delighted. We spend some time deciding on the best place for it. Melda tells me that swallows like to be high up, with a perch close by and direct access to an open area where they can swoop about, gathering insects to feed their young. Also, it has to be accessible for me so that I can clean out the box each year. After circling the house searching for possibilities, we find the perfect place. We attach the nesting box to the wall of the house just to one side of the upstairs balcony, facing the meadow. Not far away, the power and phone lines cross the driveway to enter the house. Perfect: safety from predators, a perch for the swallows and access from the deck to clean out the box in the fall. Any guest staying upstairs will be asked not to go onto the deck at nesting time.

On a bright and sunny day a few weeks later, I am clipping some overgrown salal when I hear a high-pitched chittering sound—a bird call I am not familiar with. I look up to see a swallow performing marvellous aerial manoeuvres. It swoops high against the sun, instantly changes direction and drops, only to soar up to a great height in another direction, circling the house and rising again. Then it disappears over the treetops, chittering all the while. The bird seems unable to carry out this extraordinary exhibition of flight without the accompaniment of constant song. It vanishes again, only to return to continue these extraordinary aerobatics.

Now there are two swallows. Gradually, they make passes closer and closer to the nesting box, until one lands on the balcony railing for a few seconds and is off again, but not before I can identify it as a Violet-green Swallow. I am ecstatic. The birds are back two days later, repeating their performance, this time looking into and going into the box. I drop a note to Melda to tell her about the swallows and thank her again for her gift.

Not many days later, I receive a letter back from her, enclosing four small, soft white feathers, like the breast feathers of a chicken. She tells me that when the swallows start to build a nest, I am to toss the feathers into the air for them to catch and take into the box. I have a small doubt about this. The next week is cloudy, grey and raining, and the swallows don't return, but as soon as the sun is bright again, they are back swooping and soaring and constantly chittering.

I remember the feathers and take them out to the meadow. A light breeze is blowing as I throw out a feather; it floats up and across and up again. Suddenly, out of nowhere, a swallow swoops by, catches the feather in its beak with a snapping sound and takes it into the nesting box. Utterly captivated by this new-found feather caper, I laugh and toss out one feather after another like it was a sport. If the swallow misses a feather, it makes an abrupt turnaround and takes another run at it, sometimes twice, to finally catch the floating prize. Snap! I am not believing this and laugh some more. Not long after, while hiking in Woodhus Slough, south of Campbell River, I gather up a few small white feathers from beside a pond where wild waterfowl have been preening.

When I have spring visitors from Vancouver, I hand them some feathers to enjoy the sport of "feather flying." Coincidentally, a while later, I hear a CBC radio program about this very phenomenon. A biologist has done some research on swallow nests with and without feathers built into them. His discoveries are fascinating. It seems that the feathers help to insulate the nest. The warmer a baby bird is kept, the more quickly it grows, because energy is being directed towards growth rather than maintaining body temperature. The result is that the birds are able to fledge sooner and the parent birds have to spend less time capturing food to feed the young, which may number five or six. I wonder: When did the first swallow build the first feather into its nest? And how did it communicate the idea to fellow swallows?

SWALLOWS' NEST

The parent swallows, one or both, enjoy sitting on the power line and are not bothered by activity going on beneath them. They always face in the same direction, which, I think, may be to face the sun or to keep watch on the nesting box.

Before the young fledge, they spend considerable time just peering out of the 2.5-cm (1-inch) hole in the box, surveying the wide world, waiting to feel ready to take that first plunge into the abyss of open space in front of them. Three weeks after I am sure they have all flown, I open up the nesting box to clean it out. For some reason, I am not prepared for a rectangular nest; it's 15 by 7.7 cm (6 by 3 inches). The mix of grass and feathers is about 7 cm (nearly 3 inches) thick, with a small cup-shaped hollow taking up half the rectangle. The feathers are tucked in throughout the entire nest, but a few of the larger curved ones bend over the egg cavity, like a soft white throw.

The following May, my gardening is interrupted by that familiar chittering sound. "They're back," I tell myself and look up to see two swallows chasing another pair at a fast and furious pace around the house, across the meadow, over the trees and out of sight. I watch in amazement at the rivalry for the nesting box. Finally, one pair leaves for good and the other begins nest building, so I bring out the feathers. If I delay in tossing up a feather, the bird circles around me expectantly, but instead of going directly to the box with its

VIOLET-GREEN SWALLOWS

3 4

PILEATED
WOODPECKER

prize, it first flies around the area two or three times. This must be a different pair of Violet-greens from last year; their behaviour is different. But it could be their offspring. Next season I will add another nesting box.

Each spring, the swallows return—either the original birds or their offspring—and each spring I enjoy the fun of tossing out feathers to ride the breeze, to have these marvels of flight snap them up and take them to the nest. One year, I don't see much of the swallows and surmise it is because I have been away. But at the end of the summer, when I open the nesting box to clean it out, I am saddened to see six tiny white eggs in a perfect circle—unhatched.

Spring and early summer bring many birds to the feeder that I have hung on a large tree stump that is visible from the kitchen and dining room windows—birds that I never saw in the city. There is the Golden-crowned Sparrow, similar to the everyday sparrow of city gardens but glorified by a bright golden crown atop a band of black above and below the eyes. The tap-tap-tap of a black-and-white bird pecking at the old stump sends me to my bird book. Looking at its all-white back, white flashes on its head and large bill, I identify it as a Hairy Woodpecker. And the bright red patch at the back of its head

GOLDEN-CROWNED SPARROW

indicates it is a male. Disturbed by something, he flies from the stump with a chattering, rattling call, something like that of a kingfisher. Surely the most surprising and dramatic of the woodpeckers is the large (crow-sized) Pileated, unmistakable because of its size, elongated shape and colour. This flamboyant bird is mainly black: males have a red crest on the head and red "whiskers" stripes behind the eye. When it flies, the broad, sweeping wings flash white on the undersides. One day, two of these ostentatious birds land on the tree stump and begin to circle it round and around, appearing and disappearing like horses on a merry-go-round. Fascinated, I watch until they fly off in flashy vainglory. Later, one of them returns and uses its strong chisel-shaped beak to pry off long pieces of the rotting stump, leaving a pile of debris in the flower bed below. I am very glad to have these bright birds around, but I do wish they would attack the numerous old and rotting tree trunks in the woods. This particular tree stump is the focal point of the flower bed I am creating around it. The stump is topped with a thick mound of moss, from which grow a huckleberry bush and salal. Its base is flared, and a few stalks of evergreen salal nestle artistically between two of the flares. Because the land around the tree stump slopes, I want to make a freeform, four-tiered flower bed around and beyond it.

Each time I see squarish or rectangular rocks by the roadside, I stop and heave them into my hatch-back. On one outing, I happen to find a place where a new road has been blasted through a rocky area, creating a rich source of rocks for my flower bed. It necessitates travelling over a vicious, rocky, potholed road used by logging trucks, where gullies are bridged by massive tree trunks covered over with chunky, broken rocks. My little car doesn't take kindly to this. Eventually, the flower bed, filled with enriched soil, is complete. In it, I plant two rhododendrons, one from a four-inch pot given to me by the weavers guild in Victoria, after I had delivered a lecture on Northwest Coast aboriginal weaving methods.

I also choose a variety of bedding plants which, the magazines and garden centres assure me, the deer will not eat; lobelia, alyssum, Nicotiana, snapdragon, Dusty Miller and more. As long as it is summer with plenty of wild edibles abounding, the deer leave my bedding plants alone—more or less. Garden centres offer chemical sprays to keep off deer, and magazines offer tips like "hang bars of soap from your shrubs" or "sprinkle human or dog hair in the flower beds" or "spread mothballs around your garden." Any kind of spray, organic or not, will wash off with a good rain, however; and I can't picture my flower beds with bars of soap dangling everywhere or scattered with mothballs. Since my haircut provides less than a handful of hair and I don't have a dog, that deterrent is not feasible either. Somehow we will learn to get along, the deer and I.

The funny thing about deer, I am to find out, is that their tastes change with the years; or perhaps new deer with different tastes come along. Plants that they haven't nibbled for years suddenly become Caesar salad, and during a hard winter, with snow on the ground for more than a few days, they will eat anything at all they can reach.

Many good Vancouver friends come up to Quadra to visit or to stay, and some of them are put to work. Bill often breaks his journey going to or from the Queen Charlotte Islands, and Donna and Marshall Soules visit and pitch in. While Donna works on a protective stone embankment along a drainage ditch by the driveway, Marshall is up on the roof, cleaning gutters filled with conifer needles and maple leaves. Later, Peter and Anne come to stay for a while. Typically, Peter handles a variety of "things that need doing," like checking my car, fixing a cupboard door, transplanting a tree, stacking firewood and installing weatherstripping on a door. Though they have nine acres on a small lake in the Okanagan, with superb vistas and the sound of howling coyotes at night, they miss the salt tang of the sea, the sound of waves breaking on the beach, and the sight of scudding sailboats heeling to starboard.

The three of us walk the beach together. An assemblage of seaweeds raked ashore by wind and tide lie in long tangled ropes at the high-tide line. I pull the salt-scented, wet and shiny sea growth bundles apart and pick out fragments of those species that will press well, laying them in a plastic bag from my jeans pocket. Later, I will make greeting cards from these colourful sea gems. Every outdoor jacket, coat or pants pocket holds a plastic bag or two, because there is almost always something wonderful and intriguing to bring home: either to press, identify, collect, study, transplant—or eat.

I press small flat-leaved seaweeds in the pages of old Vancouver phone books; and in the Yellow Pages, I press various wildflowers, leaves and grasses—alphabetically, so finding them again is quick and easy. Then I glue one or more pressed seaweeds or plants onto heavy paper to make greeting or note cards. Sometimes I use oil-based inks to print directly from the plants onto cards. No two prints are ever the same.

The flowers of the delicate white Queen Anne's Lace make a stunning starburst design on a dark background. My friend Joy touches them with gold paint for a glorious Christmas-card star, using a rich, deep, blue background for a night sky. Wild Trailing Yellow Violets, delicate pink Bleeding Heart and salmonberry flowers also press well, along with their leaves, and they abound around the property. For a dramatic and unusual card, I use a

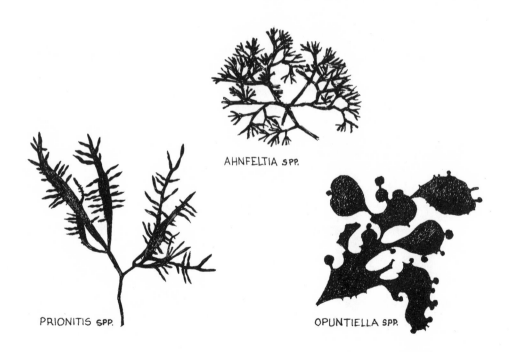

AHNFELTIA SPP.

PRIONITIS SPP.

OPUNTIELLA SPP.

TRAILING YELLOW VIOLET

BLEEDING HEART

VANILLA LEAF

skeletonized Vanilla Leaf; the large three-part leaves rot over winter, leaving behind the delicate tracings of their skeletons. Gathered fresh in summer and dried, the green leaves give out a pleasant vanillalike scent that keeps flies away—handy when camping.

•　　•　　•

I transplant a gift of Wild Ginger to the shady side of my house and eagerly watch for its extraordinary three-petalled, purply brown flowers, like something from the tropics rather than a rain-forest island. The flowers hide beneath the plant's large, heart-shaped, leathery looking leaves; the roots provide a fine ginger flavouring. Another transplant is Maidenhair Fern, that lover of moist shady places, a delicate light green plant that displays itself, leaf by multiple leaf, often cascading down rocky bluffs where water seeps. I make a semicircle of it on the shady side of a large patch of salal, echoing the contour that the evergreen shrub has taken.

In the centre of this patch is an upright beach log topped with a pottery dish, a much-used birdbath, year round. On day, when I pick up the dish to wash and refill it, I rejoice to find a Pacific Tree Frog underneath. It is crouched in a sloping area on the log top, with just enough room for it to find a cool moist place. The bright green shining body, blotched with brown, provides perfect camouflage when it clambers up shrubs and trees or moves from one branch to another. The adhesive pads on its toes allow it to cling to smooth surfaces like salal leaves.

We look at each other, frog and I, then decide we are no threat to the other. But when I return with the refilled dish, frog has hopped it. However, it's there again next morning, though now in a brownish guise, perhaps the better to blend in with the wood stump so that I won't notice it. But after several days of rude disturbance and discovery whenever I remove the dish to refill it, frog decides to find a more peaceful resting place and hops off into its green and brown jungle world, never to return. I do, however, often hear a tree frog's call some distance away; and imitating it, I get a reply. The two of us call back and forth until I give up and get on with garden work.

I have always had a soft spot for amphibians, beginning at the tender age of four. While my mother was entertaining friends for tea one afternoon, I was playing with my siblings by a small stream which ran through our property. It was there that I discovered a host of tiny green frogs and was entranced by them. Overjoyed by this wonderful new discovery, I scooped up as many as I could and ran to the house, holding my treasure in my cupped hands. Bursting into the drawing room with complete disregard for the elegantly dressed ladies sipping tea, I rushed up to my mother, eagerly exclaiming, "Look, look at the little darlings!"

I opened up my hands to show her my amazing find, which promptly allowed all the frogs to make a fast getaway from their clammy prison. They hopped off in every direction amid

WILD GINGER

spilled tea and screeches of horror from my mother's guests as I tried frantically to gather them up again. With only half a handful of frogs, I returned to the stream, disappointed that no one shared my joy in these little darlings—least of all my mother.

Many, many years later, when I was living in Vancouver, I kept a large terrarium landscaped with rocks, ferns, moss and open areas of shallow water. Over the years, it held frogs, toads, salamanders, newts and small snakes. At one time, it had a Tiger Salamander, beautifully mottled black and yellow, brought back from a camping trip in the Okanagan. They all ate meal worms, which I raised for them, or insects, which I collected.

PACIFIC TREE FROG ON SALAL LEAF

Coming face to face with the birdbath tree frog (which was at one time called a toad) not only reminds me of long ago years but of a poem that never fails to amuse and enchant me, called "A Three-Toed Tree Toad's Ode."

A he-toad loved a she-toad
That lived high in a tree.
She was a two-toed tree toad,
But a three-toed toad was he.
The three-toed tree toad tried to win
The she-toad's nuptial nod,
For the three-toed tree toad loved the road
The two-toed tree toad trod.
Hard as the three-toed tree toad tried,
He could not reach her limb;

From her tree toad bower
With her veto power—
The she-toad vetoed him.

The words roll and frolic around the tongue even as they build a touching little scenario. Surprisingly, this poem, which seems so contemporary, was written in 1892. The writer, modestly or for some personal reason, signed it Anon. A pity.

Chapter 3

On Fine Spring Mornings

JULY 1992

Mornings, I enjoy sitting out on the deck having cof-fee in the sun, alone or with a friend, to breathe in

the greenness, the softness, the leafiness, the stillness and the heady aroma of it all. Song Sparrows are perched somewhere on a branch, unseen. One is proclaiming its territorial rights with prolonged trills and a broad range of high notes, interspersed with lower notes followed by more trilling in a nonstop aria filled with the fervour of a Hallelujah chorus. Surely this bird could compete with a lark and not feel inferior. Other birds proclaim the joy of mating and join in the rich chorus of declaration of spring, morning after morning. I listen with an overpowering happiness, feeling that I should applaud such a glorious performance.

Looking around, I realize my deck looks somewhat bare and decide that three planters filled with a profusion of flowers will work wonders. I head over to the garden supply store in "the River" (no garden shop then on Quadra) and buy three large oak half-barrels as well as several sacks of soil which promise to grow flowers in abundance enough to make me the envy of my neighbours. With some effort, I wrestle these bulky and very heavy purchases into my hatch-back. Once I'm home, I have to haul out the barrels and sacks, and roll them one at a time up the four split-log steps to the deck. Then I fill the tubs and add the bedding plants bought from the local hardware store.

Later, the thought crosses my mind that perhaps I should have planted lush lettuce and leeks in the tubs, as they're out of reach of the deer. But when I discover slugs, snails and sow bugs appreciating the moist shade beneath the tubs, I am content with seedlings that will provide a riot of colourful flowers. Not that these will be immune, either. I have heard big-name gardeners on the radio saying that banana slugs eat only decaying vegetation. Yet several times I have caught them red-handed—or rather green-mouthed—gulping down fresh green leaves.

Slugs are also tipplers with a taste for beer; any brand will do. Too often when I pick up a discarded beer can (along with other litter) from the grass-edged island roads, I discover one or several slugs in their roadside "pub." In fact, beer is a well-known slug remedy—sink open cottage cheese cartons full of beer into flower beds where the slugs will drink and drown—but the method is definitely deficient in garden aesthetics. Fortunately, I learn about the perfect environmentally friendly answer, but I admit it may not be for everybody. A gardener on Cortes Island reveals the secret: a snake pit. I know many people revile and fear snakes far more than slugs, even the harmless garter snakes found in gardens, but this is an unfair evaluation of a valuable and beneficial creature. The best part is that these snakes eat slugs. So I build not one but two snake pits, some distance apart. One is simply a good-sized pile of wood, sawn up from a blow-down. The other is a pile of rocks with hollows in the earth beneath. These are safe places for a snake to hide, shelter and give birth to live young, up to twenty at a time. Twice when I raise a large flat rock, a snake is there.

BANANA SLUG

Garter snakes are really quite beautiful and diverse in colouring. Almost all of them have three light stripes running their full length, one in the centre of the back with another at each side. These may be yellow to greenish-yellow, or a bluish to greyish shade. Between the stripes, the colouring is dark brown to black.

GARTER SNAKE

The first year after creating the snake pits, I find far fewer slugs than previously, and I more frequently see a snake sunning on a bank or in the long grass. One day, I discover quite a large snake with a good-sized slug half in and half out of its wide-open mouth. There is no movement. The snake is digesting the first part of the slug before devouring the rest of it. I recall that once, on a hike, I found a snake at the edge of a small pond. In its mouth was a partially devoured frog, with one of its hind legs well down the snake's throat. Both snake and frog were motionless. My first thought was to release the frog, but that would deprive the snake of its meal. Yet if I didn't release the snake's meal, the frog would be deprived of its life. For some reason now unclear, I found myself on the side of the imperilled frog. After I slowly and carefully withdrew the frog from the snake's gaping maw, the snake swam off in anger or disappointment. The frog remained motionless, its endangered leg stiff and unable to function. Carefully, I exercised the leg, gently flexing it underwater, back and forth, back and forth, for a couple of minutes until the frog, too, swam off and disappeared.

Now I am confronted with a snake/slug situation, but this time I appreciate that the snake is doing a good job and let nature take its course.

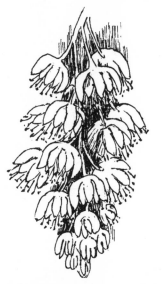

BUDDING FLOWER CLUSTER
OF BROAD-LEAFED MAPLE

On spring mornings, I am up early. The air is clean and sharp and filled with wonderful scents. Maple trees are hung with tassels of sulphur-coloured flowers and yellow greens are breaking out all over. While sweeping the deck where the corner of the roof overhangs it, providing a shaded area, I notice mouse droppings. Next morning, there are even more. Not wanting mice to slip into the house when the door is open, I set a trap baited with cheese. No takers. I switch to peanut butter, then cake. Still no takers. This is odd. There are so many droppings that I imagine a large convergence of mice in the night, but not one takes the bait.

Looking up, I see a cobweb spanning the corner where the door jamb meets the adjacent wall, and notice two droppings suspended in the gossamer web. Now I am really puzzled. Surely no mouse can walk across a cobweb without destroying it. This is a total mystery. I keep finding new droppings daily until one morning I look up again—way up. In the small space where the sloping roof corner meets the right-angled walls, I find the answer. Bats.

Hanging head down, their tiny claws hooked into the rough exterior cedar boards, are two Little Brown Myotis—bats. I am ecstatic. I don't have to trap mice, and the bats will keep down the mosquitoes.

Bats are fascinating creatures. These fur-covered mammals can fly better than many a bird. Equipped with an extraordinary sonar echolocation system, they can swiftly navigate through a forest in the dark, as well as locate flying insects, which they consume in huge quantities. When I examine the crispy dry droppings with a magnifying glass, I can make out insect legs and wings. Little Brown Myotis mate in the fall but don't give birth until early summer, to a single offspring weighing 2 g (0.07 ounce). Because the newborn must suckle frequently, possibly it may cling tightly to the mother's underside, even when she is flying.

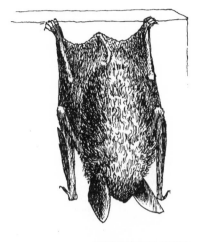

LITTLE BROWN MYOTIS

After that discovery, I look for the bats each morning. I don't see them again in daylight, but they keep leaving evidence of regular nocturnal visits. Many times I go out after dark with a flashlight to check for their presence, but only twice do I see them; the second time, there are four bats clustered together. They leave when the cool weather comes; or at least I think they are gone, until I find their droppings on the floor of an upstairs storage closet, which encloses the cement-block chimney stack of the wood stove. Somewhere, somehow, a couple of Little Brown Myotis have worked

BATS ROOSTING

their way under the cedar shakes, drawn by the warmth of the chimney. As time goes on, the droppings stop, so either the bats have migrated, as they should, or are hibernating.

Each spring I welcome the return of the bats to their hangout on my deck, and even find myself interested in a magazine article on how to build a bat house. Two years later, on a May morning, I find a hefty sprinkling of droppings; their numbers are multiplying. And twice in one week when I look under the overhang with a flashlight, I see bats.

When the island's natural history society announces a one-day workshop on moss identification, I sign up. Both the instructors are from Quadra: Daryl Rye, a retired science teacher, and Steve Mooney, a former field biologist for the British Columbia parks system. Each participant in the workshop is given a package containing pressed mosses of many different species,

OLD LOGS *with* BROOM AND ROPE MOSS

BROOM or WINDBLOWN MOSS

STEP MOSS

HAIRCAP MOSS

FAN MOSS

ROPE MOSS

CLUBMOSS

together with information on them. We also share several microscopes, the better to see and understand the intricacies of these fascinating bryophytes, which we generally take for granted or pay little heed.

In prolonged hot dry weather, most mosses turn brown, shrivel and crumble underfoot. But let it pour rain for a few days, and this special class of the plant kingdom comes into its own. Moss, in varying colours, thickly carpets the forest floor, cascades over boulders, clings to cracks in cliffs, forms deep soft tufts on rocks and logs, sheathes the trunks of trees and festoons branches. Hundreds of species of moss, each with its particular niche, contribute to the diversity of this largely moist province. I am beginning to appreciate the forest floor and its own special ecosystem more deeply than a few years ago.

The specialized knowledge of mosses shown by this young man, Steve Mooney, is impressive, and after the moss identification workshop, I ask what else interests him. With obvious enthusiasm he replies, "Everything. Absolutely everything!" In the ensuing years, I am to discover the validity of this reply. Whatever natural history question I ask Steve, he is always able to answer fully and in detail. I am constantly amazed by the scope and depth of his knowledge, be it plant, animal, fish, bird or bug. In short, "Everything."

•　　•　　•

Another fine spring morning, I am sweeping out the carport when I notice a length of straggly moss on the cement floor. A few days later, more moss. Then more. That's odd. Looking up, I see strands of moss hanging down from a crossbeam in the carport. A robin's nest is under construction, snug up against the 2 x 4, resting on the beam. While showering each morning, I look out of the bathroom window into the carport to watch the progress of the nest. Perhaps this is an inexperienced nest builder, or a very fussy one, but she abandons the beginnings of the first nest, moves over to the next 2 x 4, and starts again. When that nest is half-finished, she starts on number three, beside the next 2 x 4. This time she finishes it. The episode reminds me of the three architects and building plans before I was totally satisfied. Perhaps this robin was going through a similar process. Finally, she sits on nest number three and lays eggs. Each morning, I look to see if she is there, and one morning a small head with a huge open beak rises above the nest edge and squawks for breakfast. Then two, three and soon four hungry young cry for food and keep the robin busy much of the day.

But one day when I check, I am devastated to see the nest has gone. I dress hurriedly and go out to investigate. The nest is on the carport floor, upside-down and empty; not far away is a large smear of blood. Raccoon. A stealthy attack in the night. There are fresh claw scratches on the post closest to the nest. The predator had a feast that night. My friend Mary, who lives down the road, says that raccoons readily climb up the tall posts supporting her deck, which overhangs a rocky bluff. She has put long sheet-metal guards around the posts to stop them, but somehow they still manage to climb up. Charming, cute and funny though they are, they are rascals, and like two year olds or puppies, they get into everything everywhere, and can create havoc.

Birds can and do sometimes nest in strange places. My auto mechanic, Dennis Young, points to a robin nesting in a deep- freeze basket hanging at the back of an open-fronted storage shed next to his repair shop. The bird ignores the comings and goings of people and vehicles.

ROBIN NESTING IN CARPORT

One day, as I board the ferry to Campbell River, a flutter of grey wings in the boat's superstructure, high above the cars, catches my eye. Pigeons, and they are making a nest. The site they have chosen is sheltered from wind and rain and totally out of reach of predators. Smart birds. Before we sail, one pigeon flies off the ferry and returns with twigs to add to the nest; it even manages a second trip to shore to fetch more twigs. During the twelve-minute crossing time, the bird fusses with the nest. As soon as the ferry pulls into the dock at Campbell River, away goes the pigeon in search of more building material for its maritime mobile home.

An hour later, my shopping done, I board the ferry to return to Quadra. And there's the pigeon, with twigs in its beak, flying over the loading cars to reach its nest site. Obviously, building is still in progress, and a few minutes later off goes the bird once again. Meanwhile, the loading ramp is raised and the ferry pulls away from the dock. We are some distance out when I notice the pigeon—more twigs in beak—winging its way toward the stern of the ferry, flying as fast as it can against the wind. I can see that the bird is falling further and further behind. Eventually, it gives up, turns around and flies back to shore. I have to feel some sympathy for the pigeon; I know too well that feeling of having just missed the ferry.

Some days later, I watch another of nature's creatures collecting nesting material—but this time at my expense. I am out on the deck eating lunch when I see a wasp land on one of the peeled logs which support the roof beams. I walk over and watch it slowly back down the post, then move to another part of it, and back down again. Taking a closer look, I realize that the wasp is removing a very fine layer of wood, rolling it into a ball as it does. Now I can see that the post is covered with vertical streaks of light brown, where the weathered grey surface of the wood has been removed, mostly on the sunny side. Here and there on the post are tiny balls of the fibre, apparently abandoned.

I know that wasps and hornets chew up the fibres they collect with a type of saliva to make paperlike material for their nests, but I don't know how they peel or scrape it off. When I get near enough to the insect to zero in on it with an eye loupe, it flies off. The insect books I consult do not explain the wood-gathering process, so I ask Steve Mooney. He explains that the wasp employs a "cut and pinch" technique, using its mandibles and two pairs of labial palps (small appendages at each side of its head). The wasp uses the former to cut the fibre, and the latter to remove and manipulate it into a ball.

I am intrigued and amused by the idea that part of Hilary's house will become part of a wasp's nest. It's not long before I realize that our association is closer than I had thought. The hornet is building its nest under the roof overhang, only a short distance from where the bats hang out. Soon, there is a second nest under construction. I guess this is called "being close to nature."

I drive down to Vancouver International Airport to meet my only and special sister, Heather, flying in from her home in the village of Old Basing in Hampshire, England. She is fascinated by the small ferry that takes us over to Quadra Island, and by the fishboats and net lofts in Quathiaski Cove. As

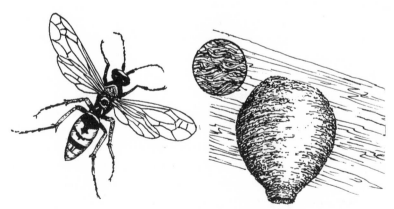

POLISTES WASP. 16mm. [⅝"] and NEST. 7·5 cm. [3"]
INSET : FIBROUS PULP LAID
DOWN IN WAVY ROWS

TWINS IN THE MEADOW

we enter my driveway, a deer and two fawns look up in welcome. I couldn't have planned it better.

Our homes are very different; Heather's is a 106-year-old heritage stone cottage with a slate-tiled roof. It's on a narrow winding road, simply called "The Street," which has several houses of great antiquity with artistically thatched roofs; one of the houses is over four hundred years old. They all have beautiful and well-kept gardens.

Old Basing has archaeological remains from Cromwellian times, and Heather once dug up a small cannonball in her garden. Similarly, while digging in my garden, I unearthed a "pebble tool," which could be several thousand years old. Its edge had been specially flaked to form a cutting or hacking edge; edges were flaked in various ways to make pebble tools for different uses.

Heather enjoys the very different lifestyle that Quadra Island offers. Having been a make-up supervisor for BBC television in England for many years, she gives a talk with memorable demonstrations of how to fake ghastly bloody wounds and burn blisters as a fund-raiser for the island's Community Centre.

ARTIFACTS FOUND ON QUADRA I.

PEBBLE TOOL, HAND MAUL, SPEAR POINT, SPINDLE WHORL
AND TWO NEPHRITE CELTS [ADZE OR CHISEL BLADES]

ALL EXCEPT PEBBLE TOOL COURTESY KWAGIULTH MUSEUM.

• • •

Many things seem to happen in the morning. I am sitting on the deck having my usual coffee, facing south to the edge of the jungled forest. The sweeping fanlike branches of hemlock create a screen, blocking my view of what's beyond, but there is a small opening that provides a glimpse of tree trunks bristling with the spindly branches that die off for lack of light as the tree grows taller. With long-handled clippers, I trim back a lot of the low hemlock branches, and then fetch my small axe to chop off all the dead branches, as far up as I can reach. One whack and a branch flies off. Whack, whack, whack, until the trunks are cleared of all that dead wood. I haul out two blow-downs, their roots long since rotted, and return to the deck to check the results.

I am thrilled with my work. Now I can see into the forest. It has depth, it's no longer a solid wall of green creating a boundary. I spend the next day working to open up this new vista, but it soon becomes clear that I need the help of a professional.

Two days later, I see a business card on the food store's public notice board, advertising J & B Tree Felling. I phone. A tall, brawny young man with a bright smile, Jerry, arrives with a large chainsaw and a beat-up truck that can go anywhere. Much of the time, I stand on the deck choosing which trees need to go: the ones that block the winter sun, the poorly grown skinny ones and some big lower branches.

Jerry asks, "How about this tree? It has a bent trunk."

"No, I like the bent trunk," I say. "Take the one beside it."

The chainsaw screams. Jerry loads up the truck with a huge pile of cut branches, bounces it over the uneven ground, and adds the debris to the burn pile he has going. He bucks up the tree trunks for firewood. At the end of the day, there is a wonderful difference to the land. He suggests felling a tall tree to further widen the gap between two forested areas, but I

CLEARING THE OVERGROWN JUNGLE

56

am undecided. It would certainly open up the vista, yet I am reluctant, for it's a fine hemlock. The decision is made for me when, a week later, a strong wind sends it crashing down. Turns out it has root rot.

As summer proceeds, I check which trees shade the deck, and when. Eventually, I have Jerry come back for further specific clearing.

Having spent my first summer with a dug well (also called a shallow well), I decide to replace it with a drilled (or deep) well and discuss the matter with John Sell, who will connect the water from the new well to the house. Then I contact a driller from Vancouver Island, but he won't drill unless I have a water dowser specify the exact spot. Fortunately, Quadra Island is home to Ted Davis, an experienced water dowser. I phone and we set up an appointment.

Ted is an elderly, stocky man with a lively countenance and bright eyes. He quickly walks around the house, practically sniffing the land, then stops. In front of him, he holds out an ordinary looking Y-shaped twig cut from a Spirea (Hardhack) bush, a moisture-loving plant. His hands each grasp one of the two prongs so that the stem of the Y points away from him, horizontally. I watch in silence as he advances, and very soon the end of the stick makes a sudden and strong downward turn.

"There's water here," he says. "Let's see how deep it is." He kneels on the ground and takes up a single straight stick, also Spirea, about 60 cm (2 feet) long. Grasping the end in both hands, one closed over the other, he points the stick out in front of him. He is still, con-centrating. Very soon the far end of the stick pulses, gently bouncing and bob-bing up and down, up and down. Ted counts the bobs; each one represents 30 cm (1 foot) down. When he stands up, he

WATER DOWSING

says, "The water is about 120 feet down. Plenty of it." Dowsing for depth is something not many people can do, he tells me, but he has been doing it for a long time.

I don't doubt there is water there, but I don't want the well head so close to the dining room window; also, it would mean uprooting some of the salal to get the drilling rig in. I express these concerns to Ted.

"Well," he says pointing, "the water likely goes in that direction, so I should find it somewhere on the other side of the house also." We move to the northwest side, and further down the sloping meadow. Ted walks across the area, holding the Y branch horizontally until the end of it suddenly snaps downward. He turns around and walks over that bit again. I am in awe. Of course, I have read about water dowsing and divining, but I have never watched it in action. Again Ted kneels, holding out the straight stick, counting the bobs with the regularity of a metronome. "Just about the same," he eventually declares. "The water's around 120 feet down." That's good news, as some wells go a lot deeper than that.

Ted drives a wooden stake tied with a red plastic ribbon into the ground where he was kneeling. He suggests that John Sell may want to connect the waterline of the new well with that of the old pipe coming up from the pump house, some distance away. When I explain that I don't really know where it comes into the house, he says, "Oh well, I'll find out." Within minutes, he locates the pipe and finds the depth.

I am intrigued. Curious as to whether or not I might have the ability to dowse, I ask Ted if I can try. "Sure," he says, and shows me how to hold the Y stick firmly but lightly. I walk over the flagged area and back. No response. I try again. Not a flicker of movement. I ask Ted if I can put my hands over his and try once more. He suggests that we share the stick, so we each take one side of the forked end and walk over the flagged area, slowly. Suddenly, I feel a powerful tug and the Spirea branch tilts sharply downward, almost pulling away from my hand—but the power of the pull was not from my side.

In answer to my questions, Ted says he has had the ability to dowse for around fifty years, but it was only nine years ago that he "put out a shingle" and began doing it professionally. While not wishing to disclose all his professional secrets, he does tell me that dowsing is partly a matter of deep concentration; he is "wired into it" and channels his energy to sensing water. As for determining the depth with a single stick, he says that the greater the amount of water, the faster the pulse, or the bounce, of the stick. In addition to water, he can also find other things, such as a lost penknife in the grass. I feel privileged to have had a personal encounter with water dowsing, and to have met this rather special person.

A week later, the drilling rig arrives. After a couple of days of clanging and thumping and spewing muddy water; of long steel pipe clunking and banging and being welded together; and after layers of sand, clay, pebbles and mud are strewn all around in a dreadful mess, the well is capped at 129 feet. It provides 54.5 L (12 gallons) a minute.

Next, an excavator digs a deep trench from the well head to the house. John Sell then takes over and lowers an electric pump to the bottom of the well; he runs pipe and power along the trench to the house, through the crawl space and up into a storage area under the stairs. There, he also installs a pressure tank, which means that when there are power outages, I will still be able to draw a quantity of water, both hot and cold. No more having to keep water in the fridge for emergencies. No more having to carry bath water out to the plants. The old pump house, far down the driveway and in the woods, becomes a storage shed for snow tires along with bundles of newspapers and bags of recyclable materials.

I am in my favourite reading corner, working on the final details of the book on totem poles, when my train of thought is suddenly shunted by what sounds like a jackhammer on the roof right above me. RAT-A-TAT-TAT-TAT-TAT-TAT. The house has a cathedral ceiling and hence no attic, so the sound is sharp, clear and very loud. I am stunned and curious. Again RAT-A-TAT-TAT-TAT-TAT-TAT, just like the road repairman's pneumatic drill that I would watch in amazement when I was a kid. Each burst of roof-drilling lasts only about one second. What is it?

I put down my work and go out onto the deck to see who or what is on my roof. And there is the source of all the noise—a Red-shafted Flicker

RED-SHAFTED FLICKER

perched on the far end of the roof peak. It spots me and flies off, flashing its white back and the orangey-red undersides of its wings and tail. It is a beautiful bird, bigger than a robin, but my heart sinks. This flicker is a woodpecker, I know, so there must be some kind of insect living in, or no doubt boring into, the hand-spilt cedar roof shakes. I don't dare contemplate what a new roof is going to cost.

The next day, the flicker is back. Two days later, I run into Larry, one of the men who built my house. I tell him about the problem and ask if he thinks I have termites, teredos or some other terrible infestation in the roof. Smiling, he explains that the flicker was in fact drumming, not drilling. This seems to be a communication sound associated with mating or territorial rights. The bird's beak does not even pierce the shakes, and there certainly aren't any colonies of insects.

Extremely relieved, I return to my work, happy to accept that such encounters with untamed creatures come with the territory. It's island.

Chapter 4

Summer Roving and Boating

While some of my visitors spend time helping in the garden or on an ongoing project, we inevitably end up going for a walk on the beach. Many of the beaches have hardly any sand, so we walk on wave-washed pebbles and stones. Huge boulders often sit at the low tide's edge where they stand out, black and bold, offering perches to gulls, eagles and cormorants. The high-tide line is rimmed with a tangle of beach logs, writhing tree roots, log butts and masses of other assorted wood debris.

Visitors take pleasure in discovering and taking home some sea gems found along a beach. For me, it is second nature to always be scanning the beach, the sea, the distant islands and Coast Mountains, the sky, the upper shore's edge, the trees and bushes—checking it all out for something of interest. Not all sea gems and finds are for the pocket, though.

After a morning spent gardening, my Vancouver friend Terre Thom and I go beach walking on the east side of the island. Ahead of us is a large dead seal; three Bald Eagles are feasting on it, but they fly off as we get too close. Someone has slit the body all the way down one side, and the eye on the upper side has been taken by eagles or vultures, which have also started pecking at the flesh beneath the layers of fat exposed by the slit. It must have been killed by a fish farmer. Fish farmers aren't fond of seals for obvious reasons; after shooting a seal, they slit it so the body will sink.

Hair Seals (also called Harbour Seals) frequently swim along Quadra's coast close to the beaches, and the tops of their heads can be mistaken for kelp bulbs. These sea mammals are especially abundant in March, when schools of herring, a choice food for them, arrive to spawn in large tidal pools. The seals have favourite rocks for hauling out and resting, often numbers of them together. When danger threatens, they wriggle themselves back into the security of the sea.

Next, we find a big patch of Bull Kelp that looks like a giant sea serving of spaghetti, tangled and twisted. Bull Kelp likes swift-flowing waters, so all this has been washed in from somewhere, after a storm ripped it free of the rocks. Kelp clings to a rock with its "holdfast," which resembles a cluster of roots, growing in size as the kelp grows. A long brown stalklike stipe, which can reach up to 30 m (about 100 feet) in length, ends in a hollow bulb. The bulb contains carbon monoxide, which allows it to float upwards, and from it grow two long, slender clusters of leaflike blades. At high tide, kelp can be well under water, but at low tide it can form big mats that float on the water's surface and present a hazard to small boat propellers. While small fish find protection among the kelp blades, some canny birds use the floating mat as a jetty from which to catch dinner.

Aboriginal people found several uses for this versatile seaweed. To make long strong fishing lines for catching halibut, fishermen stretched, twisted and dried lengths of the solid portion of the kelp stipe, then tied several lengths together for deep-sea fishing. The hollow part of the stipe was cut off and used to store eulachon oil; after plugging the open end, the stipe was coiled and hung on the house wall. A useful funnel was made by slicing off the top half of a kelp bulb and cutting off the stipe just below it.

There are other uses for kelp, too. I once watched a woman, a musician, cut off a section of the thick hollow stipe, make holes along the length, then partially plug one end. She played it like a flute, and it sounded great.

Among the beach kelp are other seaweeds torn from rocks by the power of a storm-tossed sea. The brilliant green Sea Lettuce, translucent and paper thin, also attaches itself to rocks, but fairly high up the beach. In rough weather, it readily breaks loose, so there is often a lot of it at the high-tide line. Picked fresh off the rocks, Sea Lettuce is quite edible: boil it in water for a couple of minutes, drain, then serve with butter and a dash of

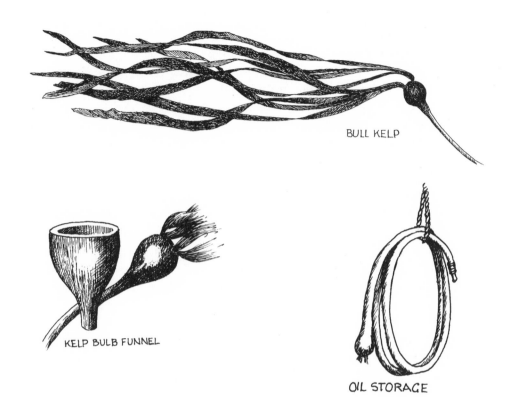

BULL KELP

KELP BULB FUNNEL

OIL STORAGE

BLADDER WRACK

SEA LETTUCE

vinegar. Or dry and store it to crumble over food for seasoning.

Abundant among the ragged ribbon of displaced seaweeds tossed ashore by the tide is Bladder Wrack. Greenish-brown, tough and leathery, it has small bladders at the ends of its multiple- branched tips. As kids, we used to pinch or step on the bladders to make them pop, not knowing that one of its common names is Popping Wrack. I pull apart the heap of vegetation to look for the rarer seaweeds, or ones suitable for pressing to make greeting cards. The pungent scent of sea and decaying vegetation is rich in my nostrils as I turn the seaweeds, disturbing all manner of small critters, both the running and jumping type. Their job is to help the seaweeds to break down and rot. After picking out one seaweed for future identification, I let them get on with it. Seaweed makes excellent garden compost, but it is too heavy to for me to carry back to the car in any quantity.

Terre and I walk on with the entire beach to ourselves, following the high-tide line. I notice a big patch of blackberry bushes, the still-green fruit bending the loaded branches, and make a note of its location. In a month or so, the berries will be ripe, and I will return with collecting bags.

Not far away, sprawling over logs, are the vines of Beach Pea, with its typical pealike features. The reddish-purple and bluish flowers bloom together with the ripening pods, with each containing several peas that are quite tasty when cooked. It reminds me of when I used to take groups from Strathcona Park Lodge on "Survival in the Wilderness" camping trips. I got people to gather quantities of these peas, shelling, cooking and eating them in spite of remarks like "I always thought they were poisonous." With a touch of salt and butter, the peas were declared "Much better than canned."

Looking up, I see the black silhouette of two large birds with widespread wings,

BEACH PEA

soaring in a wide circle. But they are not eagles. They are vultures, Turkey Vultures, and they must have spotted the dead seal down the beach. With their 1.8-m (6-foot) wingspan, they can be mistaken for eagles; the difference mainly lies in the angle of the wings. An eagle glides or soars with its wings on a horizontal plane, while a vulture's wings are uplifted, forming a dihedral, or shallow V. If the vultures were not so high, we could see the featherless red flesh on the head and neck, designed for thrusting into a carcass. Unlike the eagle with its sharp staccato cry, the vulture has no call at all.

TURKEY VULTURE

Further along the beach, stranded between high- and low-tide levels, sits a gigantic tree stump on its side, the sprawling network of roots soaring at least 4 m (12 feet) into the air. The diameter of the stump is probably 1.5 m (5 feet). The flat top indicates that the tree was logged before the stump was washed out and carried downriver to the sea. Now the great stump sits on the wide deserted beach like a monumental sculpture: bold yet intri-

BALD EAGLE *and* TURKEY VULTURE

65

cate, balanced, dramatic and powerful, worthy of any sculpture exhibit. How long, I wonder, since this stump was a seedling emerging from the pungent humus of the forest floor somewhere up the coast? How long did it thrive and what height did it attain before the deep bite of a chainsaw sent it crashing? How far has the stump drifted with wind and current? We walk over for a closer look. Someone else has appreciated its sculptural quality and even embellished it: at the stump's base is a well-arranged group of chunks of old iron, twisted and rusted.

A frantic high-pitched rattling cry draws our attention shoreward. Swooping down from a tree is a Belted Kingfisher. For its body size it has a big head, topped with a ragged crest. Mostly grey, it has a white neckband and chest. The rusty red patch on the white chest indicates this one is a female. Wings beating rapidly, it hovers a moment before plunging down into a tidal pool, immediately surfacing and flying off with a small fish in its large bill.

Continuing on our way, we become conscious of a light scuffling sound ahead of us, and Terre remarks on it. "It's crabs," I say.

"But where are they?" she asks. I turn over a big stone, and five or six lit-

BELTED KINGFISHER

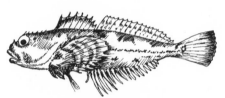

TIDEPOOL SCULPIN _ to 9 cm [3"]

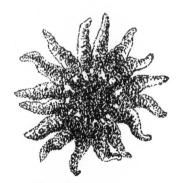

SUNFLOWER STAR

tle Purple Shore Crabs scuttle off, this way and that, to seek refuge under other stones. As long as these crabs have shade and moisture, they can stay out of the water for a considerable time, so they can be found under stones well up the beach. As we walk, the crabs are aware of our approach through sound and vibration, and hurry to hide themselves underneath stones for safety. Collectively, the sound of their scuffling is quite audible. These are the critters that raccoons relish, turning over stones to get at them and crunching them up whole.

PURPLE SHORE CRAB. 3.7cm [1½"] ACROSS BACK

After hiking for quite a way, we come to large rocks clustered along the beach. A closer look reveals a good quantity of Plate Limpets; greenish-grey and mottled, they almost seem like part of the rock. I haven't eaten limpets since a group of us roasted them on a plank, close to a fire's embers on a beach on South Moresby, in the Queen Charlotte Islands. I pull out a plastic bag from my pocket and collect some. They'll make a tasty hors d'oeuvre for dinner.

HERMIT CRAB

As soon as a limpet is touched, it clamps down so tightly that even a penknife cannot get between the shell and the rock to pry it off. The only way to take a limpet is unawares, with a swift blow to the side to dislodge the foot

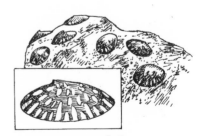

PLATE LIMPET. 4 cm [1⅗"]

that holds on so fast. Sliding a knife quickly underneath works too, but that can be hard on the blade's edge. I gather over a dozen large ones, then fill another bag with pea gravel. Back home in the kitchen, I will rinse the limpets well and lay them flesh-side up on the pea gravel in a shallow pan to prevent them from tipping over. I'll make garlic butter, stir in a bit of finely chopped parsley, and spoon a little of this mixture over each limpet. Two or three minutes under the broiler is all they will need.

As we retrace our steps, Terre finds an exquisite pebble, black with intrusions forming an artistic pattern; she also picks up a long slender feather which appears to be from a heron's wing. Keepers both.

In my city days, my brother, friends and I made the most of every weekend, especially three-day weekends. If we didn't go sailing, riding or camping, we'd load our canoes atop the car and head for some lake, preferably a lesser known one reached by a backroad. So when Pete and Sophie Gregg suggest I join them for a day of canoeing on Quadra, I don't hesitate. My friend Terre, visiting with me, is also welcomed.

The Greggs are keen outdoors people and love to canoe. Some years ago, Pete invented an ingenious rig to ease the effort required for long-distance or all-day paddling, though it is limited to the double paddle. Called a "Paddle Pal," the whole thing looks so simple that I want to try it out, but we won't be needing a double paddle this day, so leave it for another time.

We load two canoes on top of Pete's van and drive north to Village Bay Lake. There, we launch the canoes from a beach beside the bridge that crosses a narrow neck of the lake. After paddling past a scattering of summer cottages along the shore, we reach a channel that becomes narrower and shallower, until the canoes are sliding through a bed of tall reeds that rattle against the hulls. This is ideal Red-Wing Blackbird territory, but it is the wrong time of year for nesting.

The channel opens out into Mine Lake, and we pass a large sloping point of rock perfectly mirrored in the still water. Eventually, we pull up to a tiny sandy beach that is one of the few places here to make a landing, to rest and eat our lunch.

ON MAIN LAKE

Continuing on after our break, utter beauty and peace prevail, with only the gurgle of the paddles slicing the water to break the silence—until two loons call back and forth to each other. The sounds spread over the lake, filling the quiet with echoes of their eerie call. High in the sky, three eagles soar in sweeping circles. We paddle on without speaking, reluctant to shatter the perfect splendour with unneeded words, taking in and appreciating all that surrounds us.

A narrowing of the lake leads into a third body of water, Main Lake, where we find some friends of the Greggs, camping on a small beach. We visit with them for a while and swim in the warm clear water.

Heading west reveals a vista of mountain peaks and a small island. We paddle close to the shore, which is mostly a tangle of vegetation, swamped logs and reeds, on the lookout for any wildlife. Sophie recalls once seeing a throng of frogs on a log and a Saw-Whet Owl on a branch, but we only intrude on a pair of ducks that dive for safety before we can figure out what kind they are.

Early evening brings us to a rock bluff with a bay to one side, the perfect place to beach our canoes. We light a small fire on the rock and cook up supper, then paddle back to the bridge on Village Bay Lake and drive home.

Another time, I do try out the Paddle Pal, a great help to the canoeist or kayaker. Pete's simple and adjustable rig has a paddle suspended on a flexible cord, rendering it weightless when in use, yet permitting it to rotate freely. The rig is certainly a benefit to the young and healthy, but it is a special boon to anyone with wrist, arm or shoulder problems. And he has patented it in both Canada and the United States.

My anthropologist friend, Joy Inglis, has long been interested in the many petroglyphs which abound on Quadra Island's shores. So has Marcia Wolter, a long-time resident on the island. Together, they have been recording, through photos and rubbings, these ancient designs and symbols grooved into large and small boulders by Quadra's early First Nations inhabitants. Over many years, Joy has done much research on petroglyphs, seeking to define the technology and the designs, as well as the social and spiritual interpretations and values of this early stone art. Now she is diligently writing a book on this subject, using the petroglyphs found on Quadra in addition to some others on the coast, and has asked me to do the illustrations. It is an intriguing challenge, and I gladly accept. The challenge comes in finding a technique to portray the images of the petroglyphs precisely and completely, while keeping them visually attractive. For a variety of reasons, photography cannot always achieve all of this, yet outline drawings are not realistic either, as the black lines don't capture the feeling of rock.

At low tides and when the lighting conditions are good, Joy takes me down to the island beaches so that I can examine and experience each petroglyph, the better to understand what I will be illustrating. There are also eight petroglyph boulders in front of the Kwagiulth Museum at Cape Mudge village. Seven of them are from the beach that fronts the site of the early village of Tsa-Kwa-Luten, which was atop a sandy bluff south of Cape Mudge. The eighth boulder was moved from the beach north of the present village. There are large elaborate designs on the main face of these boulders. No designs are visible on the back or sides, but Joy wants to try a special technique for a more exacting scrutiny.

On a dark night, Joy and I drive over to the petroglyph collection by the museum. Ross Henry, an excellent island photographer, and his wife, Janice

Kenyon, join us there, bringing along a stepladder. Joy manoeuvres a powerful propane gas lantern so that the light strikes obliquely across a boulder. She moves the lantern around to light up different areas of the rock; suddenly, there is a collective cry of delight as a small face shows up through the shadows cast by the lantern. Ross positions the ladder and climbs up it to take a photo of the face. Then another such petroglyph is found, and we move from boulder to boulder, searching all sides for glyphs not visible since ancient times and seeing well-known ones in a different light, literally. It is an exciting and revealing experiment that thrills us all. Later, I work from the photographs and rubbings of these finds to make drawings of about a dozen rediscovered glyphs for Joy's book-in-progress.

REDISCOVERED PETROGLYPHS

71

Another time, a small group of us walk a short way along the pebbly beach in front of Joy and Bob's house to look at a huge granite boulder that is partially buried above the high-tide line. The large petroglyph on it depicts a Sea Wolf with a Salmon incorporated into its body. On the top of the rock are several "pits," small round cavities pounded into the stone, an often seen feature. Using a flat piece of driftwood as a shovel, we remove a quantity of storm-tossed pebbles from around the base of the rock, revealing many more pits not previously recorded. Joy is elated by the discoveries. Not far away are several much smaller rocks with other petroglyphs that she has long known about. They all look out over the northern Gulf Islands and the Coast Mountains beyond.

We climb a path up the bluff to Joy's house and relax on the deck overlooking the sea and Coast Mountains. A Bald Eagle stalks the beach for tidal tidbits while another perches high in a fir tree, digesting a meal or keeping watch, alert to anything of interest on the water. With an extraordinary visual capability, (nine times greater than that of a human), an eagle can spot a small object from a tremendous distance: a floating dead herring, for instance, will send it winging over the water.

HERRING BALL

This day we witness a marine spectacle known as a "herring ball." When a school of herring is threatened by predators in the water below them, such as a school of salmon or seals, they close up and move into a ball at the sea's surface for protection. The telltale sign of a herring ball is the splashing disturbance of surface water, which brings gulls flying in to the feast. Their wheeling, screeching, diving and splashing send a visible and audible signal to other gulls, until the birds form a white whirling cloud.

Inevitably, the gulls are joined by eagles. Leaving a favoured perch, these large, legendary birds raise powerful wings with a span of up to nearly 2.4 m (8 feet) and head for the herring ball. Strong, steady wingbeats, deliberate and unhurried, express the elegance and power of this coastal bird held in high esteem by those familiar with it. And it has always been thus. For thousands of years, First Nations people who lived along the bays, inlets, channels and islands of British Columbia's rugged and wild coast deeply revered this regal creature. They knew of its special powers, understood its place in their culture, and honoured it accordingly. Certain high-ranking lineages inherited or acquired the right to take this imposing bird as their family crest. Many still do.

A magnificent moment presents itself whenever I hear the distant, staccato notes of an eagle and look up. This time, above my house, high, high in a bright cerulean sky, six eagles are soaring, wide wings extended. "Making lazy circles in the sky" is exactly what they are doing. Drifting, circling, shifting with immobile ease, one crossing in front of another, another sliding back. Now I count eight small black silhouettes and soon there are ten, turning, wheeling, all the while rising higher and higher, still grouped in a loose circular space, suspended, floating. Are they riding a thermal for the sheer joy of it? Are they aloft to gain a vantage point for some reason? Ten or more minutes go by before the team of gliders slowly separates. The eagles drift away, leaving an empty hole in the sky and a glow in my heart.

I have been hearing about the Octopus Islands for some time, and they sound enchanting. Looking them up on a chart, I find that of the scattering of small islets off the east coast of Quadra's northern end, eight are defined as the Octopus Islands. When I hear about a Field Naturalists Society overnight trip to these islands, I sign up.

Ralph Keller of Coast Mountain Expeditions on Read Island brings his rugged 32-foot all-purpose boat, *Chico Mendes*, over to Heriot Bay on Quadra to pick up our group of a dozen or so campers. The weather is perfect, and I am eager to see the northern west coast of Quadra from the water. When we leave behind the last of the waterfront homes, the rocky coastline becomes increasingly dramatic, gouged and broken in some places, defended by high bluffs and barren rocks in others. Deep cracks and fissures in the grey stone create remarkable designs and textures, while tall trees and other vegetation crowd the edge of precipitous walls of rock.

Further north, the Discovery Islands are a close-knit collection of raggedly shaped fragments of forested land, some quite large, some small, like leftovers from creation. Read, Maurelle and Sonora Islands are clustered together in a curve, with enough space between to maintain their independence. The tide finds it difficult to pour itself through the narrower passages, and the water is turbulent, swirling in wide circles. The current grabs at the hull of the *Chico Mendes* and swings it off course, but the next moment the power of the upswelling, surging water tosses the boat in another direction. The skipper is accustomed to this unruly behaviour of the sea and keeps an upper hand. Knowing that, we can enjoy the experience of going through this slender gap between Quadra and Read, aptly named Surge Narrows.

Next, Ralph swings the flat-bottomed boat into Yeatman Bay, almost to the edge of the shelving beach. Some of us wade ashore, others he carries on his back like a latter-day St. Christopher. Though we appear to be in some remote wilderness, we are, in fact, on Quadra. We hike up a trail-cum-stream bed which was originally an early logging road, pausing at one point to gain, from Ralph, an understanding of how the ecology here has completely changed as a result of that industry.

At a swampy pool, we examine a strange underwater fungus called Swamp Beacon and also spot three Pacific Coast Newts, their orangey-yellow

PACIFIC COAST NEWT 16·5cm [6½"]

undersides contrasting with the reddish-brown of their topsides. Further on, someone finds a cluster of pinky red Pinesap pushing its way up through the forest floor. This strange-looking plant, termed a saprophyte, has no chlorophyll, nor is it parasitic, but lives on decaying organic matter.

The trail ends at Main Lake, one of a chain of three lakes, tranquil and beautiful. The stillness is broken only by a Belted Kingfisher, which shatters the bright sheet of water as it plummets down, surfacing again with a fish in its beak. In the distance, two canoes ripple the water in silence.

Back on the boat, we travel northwest, stopping to look at a pictograph on a vertical rock wall, pondering the meaning and purpose of the red-painted figures. On the right is a human face with several stripes which may indicate face paint; to the left is a fish. Ralph thinks that the high curved back and prominent dorsal fin may denote a rockfish.

Soon after, we reach our destination, the Octopus Islands, and Ralph

THE OCTOPUS ISLAND WHERE WE CAMP

NODDING ONION *and* STONE-CROP. OCTOPUS ISLS.

steers the boat into a quiet rock-backed beach. Two trips in the dinghy transfer us and all our gear ashore to a tiny island. Solid rock, it is sparsely covered with thick moss, patches of grass, a scattering of White Pines, some shrubs, wildflowers, broken shells, and goose droppings. The broken shells are a result of river otters using rocks to smash open clams and cockles to eat the flesh.

A stone hearth encircled by drift-log seating forms the camp centre, and we set up our tents on whatever flat or near-flat ground we can find. I choose a fairly grassy space at the island's edge where the rock slopes down to the water in ledges. While Ralph prepares dinner, we explore this exquisite island, finding Nodding Onion in bloom, Stone-crop with its spiky yellow flowers and the spent heads of others.

A flaming sun, streaked with wisps of dark cloud, eventually settles behind a distant mountainous island—like a gaudy cliché painting with no frame. Before the light goes, we are treated to the curious sight of a Chinese junk gently sailing past our island and off into the gathering dusk.

Morning brings sunlight pressing down onto the side of my tent, and I awake. Normally an early riser, I make a conscious decision to just lie there in my sleeping bag to savour the realization of where I am, knowing that I don't have to kindle the fire or make breakfast. Eventually, I get up, dress and unzip the tent door. There, just in front, two Canada geese and four fuzzy goslings, backlit by the early sun, casually wander by. Pausing to peck

CANADA GEESE and GOSLINGS

at something now and again, the family makes its way down the sloping rock. One by one, they plop into the sea and silently swim off. What a wonderful way to start the morning.

I walk over to the other campers standing around the fire, coffee in hand, and eagerly tell them my mother goose story.

"You should have got up earlier," one of them says. "They were all around your tent."

In the middle of the Strait of Georgia, 19 km (12 miles) southeast of Quathiaski Cove, lies a special island that is rich in flora and fauna, particularly wildflowers and seabirds. A provincial park, Mitlenatch Island, all of 36.6 ha (88 acres), enjoys a mild climate with only 75 cm (30 inches) of rain a year and is host to such desert plants as Woolly Sunflower, Great Mullein and cactus, which also flourish in the hot sunny interior of British Columbia. As much of the island is rocky, Mitlenatch supports the largest seabird colony in the Strait of Georgia.

I had visited this wondrous isle several years ago on the way to Cortes Island with Bill on his boat. At that time I was doing research for my book on aboriginal fishing methods and had focussed mainly on the remains of ancient stone fish traps in the shallow bay. So when the Campbell River Museum announces a summer excursion to Mitlenatch, to be led by a botanist, I sign up.

2nd. YEAR HERRING GULL _ *left*.
3rd. YEAR , *right*.

After several hours sailing on the 38-foot *Bonnie Belle*, built on the lines of a fishing trawler, we reach Mitlenatch and discover a large colony of seals hauled out on a rocky point. We drop anchor in Camp Bay and take the dinghy ashore. Much of the island is craggy rock, ideally suited to the nesting seabirds, and is therefore out of bounds to visitors from mid-May to mid-August. However, there is a bird-blind which offers a chance to watch colonies of gulls nesting and feeding their young. Elsewhere, well-worn trails take us over diverse plant habitats: grassy meadows, dry rocky ground, bare and mossy rock, wet areas, wooded shrubby places and a beach. I'm thrilled by the sight of so many species of wildflowers in such abundance, especially the less-often seen Tiger Lily, Death Camas, Woolly Sunflower, Harvest Brodiaea and Prickly-pear Cactus.

GLAUCOUS-WINGED GULL

Throughout the nesting season, Mitlenatch is under the guardianship of amateur but enthusiastic naturalists who volunteer, in pairs, to keep watch for two-week stretches. They stay in a very rustic

TIGER LILY

PRICKLY-PEAR CACTUS

HARVEST BRODIAEA

WOOLLY SUNFLOWER

GUMWEED

HAREBELL

DEATH CAMAS

two-room cabin (some of it made of driftwood) built up against a rockface which forms one wall of the bedroom. The two current residents make us welcome and answer all our questions. Sprawled over the rocks outside the cabin, we eat our picnic lunch, watching swallows swoop low over us. They are nesting under the overhang of the cabin's roof.

On the return trip, I realize that to fully appreciate and enjoy the diversity of this jewel of an island, it needs to be visited in all its seasons. And I make a mental note to do just that.

WARDENS' CABIN — MITLENATCH I.

LOOKING EAST FROM REBECCA SPIT

.　　.　　.

The overnight trip to the Octopus Islands has given me a good look at Quadra's northeast side. I have seen the southwest side on the way to Mitlenatch Island, and I have been over to Read Island. Yet there is much of Quadra that I have not seen, especially in the more remote north end. Then, I get the idea of chartering a boat to circumnavigate the entire island, and confer with my good friend Babs Brereton, a kindred spirit. She enthusiastically sets about finding a suitable vessel and enough people to make the shared cost reasonable. As things turn out, I am unable to go on the date arranged, but the trip proves so popular that it is repeated a month later.

The boat we charter is the *Kathrion II*, which is run by Discovery Launch Water Taxi of Campbell River. It comes over to Quathiaski Cove to pick us up and about sixteen of us climb on board. She is 31 feet long and can seat all of us under cover, though most people choose to stay outside on the aft deck. We head south down Quadra's coast past a lot of waterfront homes, past the village of Cape Mudge and past the classic white-painted, red-roofed lighthouse built in 1898. Not far beyond and up the sloping hillside is the imposing Tsa-Kwa-Luten Lodge, a resort owned and operated by the We-Wai-Kai band. The lodge takes its name from a once-important First

Nations village of the Vancouver-Comox people, near which explorer Captain George Vancouver dropped anchor in 1792. His expedition artist, William Sykes, made a detailed drawing of the village of plank houses atop the bluff, now much eroded.

After rounding the southern tip of Quadra, the boat passes Francisco Point and heads northward up the east coast. Fingers point to homes of friends, relatives or neighbours, until a stretch of unbroken foreshore gives way to Rebecca Spit, our much loved and much used provincial park. Originally an old homestead, then a military rifle range, then privately owned, the long narrow spit came into public hands in a land deal with the provincial government in 1959.

At the end of the spit, we sweep into the familiar waters of Heriot Bay and out again along inhabited shores. After sailing through the offshore Breton Islands, we go past the Dunsterville Islands and follow a stretch of bold rugged coastline, uninhabited and roadless. In the distance, on the mainland, the range of Coast Mountains capped by billowing cumulus clouds against a Prussian blue sky adds to the perfection of the scene. At Bold Point, we see a single remote house perched high on the rocks, almost the last sign of habitation along the northern coast.

HEADING TOWARD HOLE-IN-THE-WALL ~ SONORA AT LEFT, MAURELLE RIGHT

We continue on through Hoskyn Channel, which separates Quadra and Read, sailing through the Settlers Group, a cluster of mountainous islands that lie between Read and Maurelle. The powerful boat takes Surge Narrows without much problem, bringing us into Okisollo Channel. There is almost no marine traffic; a heron leisurely flies by and someone spots a seal. The skipper steers the boat through the Octopus Islands, and I recall the camping trip there.

The narrow passage that separates Maurelle from its close neighbour, Sonora Island, is called Hole-in-the-Wall. Here the water is extremely turbulent, with choppy waves, whirlpools and powerful currents and countercurrents. We head straight for it. High mountains rise on either side; it is a magnificent spot. I have often heard the name Hole-in-the-Wall without knowing what it was; now I am experiencing it. All this is followed a while later by the Upper Rapids, another body of wild water that curves around the very northern end of Quadra to the Lower Rapids, which are not quite so wild.

After rounding Granite Point, we enter Kanish Bay and pass the lovely Chained Islands, a series of small islands that hang together in a curved shape like a string of jewels. Granite-edged, pristine and sunlit, they are exquisite.

Now we come out into Discovery Passage, the large body of water between Quadra and Vancouver Island, the main route of travel up and down the British Columbia coast for freighters, cruise ships, fishboats, cruisers, anglers and anything that floats. Suddenly, it's like being on a busy freeway, with marine traffic heading in both directions. It's noisy and the air is no longer clean and fresh. Boats hurry and jostle for space, and we have to detour to avoid a fishboat setting out its seine net.

Still heading south, we enter Seymour Narrows and sail beneath the power lines that carry electricity to Quadra. In the distance ahead, I see Copper Cliffs, a high vertical wall of rock, and ask the skipper if he will take us closer. As the cliffs loom up, I can make out large patches of yellowish-bronze lichen and suspect it might be the source of the cliff's name. I am wrong. Nearer now, I can see a series of brilliant turquoise-coloured patches and streaks, evidence of copper. The tremendous high wall of stone

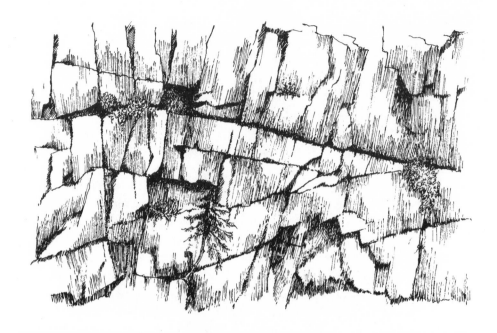

is slashed with fissures and cracks—horizontal, vertical and sometimes diagonal—as well as with ledges and ridges. A variety of vegetation clings to whatever foothold it can find, and flourishes. The entire wall is a stunning canvas of pattern and colour, constantly and subtly changing as the boat slowly moves along.

With Copper Cliffs behind us, we pass Gowlland Island and April Point Lodge and its wharfs on the tip of April Point. Since its humble beginnings in the 1940s, the lodge has grown into a world-famous fishing resort and marina.

Finally, after four hours on the water, we complete the circumnavigation of Quadra and return to dock at Quathiaski Cove. I feel that I know the island much better than before and have a better appreciation of how beautiful and varied it really is.

Chapter 5

Creatures Great and Small

...HEADS ALL TURNED TOWARD ME, ARE
FOUR MASKED BANDITS...

From time to time, I walk around my property and consider it from various aspects. There is one eyesore that I wish I could do something about: an enormous, overgrown pile of old rotten stumps and logs, a legacy from when the property was partially logged and cleared for the McTavishes' mobile home and horse pasture. I resign myself to the fact that it is there to stay. Or is it? I contact Doug of Doug Peters Excavating and ask if it would be possible to clear away the whole mess. He comes over to check on it, and yes, he could remove it all and grade the surface.

Next week, Doug's excavator growls and grinds, picking up the huge old rotting logs and stumps, and dropping them into his big truck. When the truck is full, he drives off to dump the contents at a fill site—four truck-loads, piled high, before the land can be smoothed over. What a transfor-mation! It's like reclaiming lost land. I am so elated with the way it improves the surroundings that I bring Doug back to clear other areas that are over-run with tangled profusions of salal, salmonberries, scrub alder and brack-en. All this opens up the meadow and enhances the treed areas. Doug com-pletes his work by clearing an area on the treed south edge of the property, an area so jungly and unkempt that at times I have considered disclaiming ownership.

Now it's again time to mow the grass near the house. I have been using a weed-eater to keep the grass short for a distance of 12 m (40 feet), which is as far as the electrical cord reaches from the outlets on the deck. The rest of the meadow waves in long grass which turns brown in hot summer weath-er. But having broken my right arm (a fall on the ice) while spending Christmas with friends at Whistler in the mountains, I find it is still not strong enough to handle the weed-eater for any length of time. I bring in Bill Williams, with his fast and efficient ride-on mower.

I seed the areas Doug has cleared, and eventually these need cutting. Bill Williams returns to cut the grass again, and I keep moving the uncut boundary each time he comes, so that before long he is cutting the entire grass area except for small islands around large trees and the big lupin patch. And I like it. More birds, especially robins, spend time in the mead-ow, searching for bugs which are now accessible to them, and Red-shafted Flickers peck deeply, aerating the ground. But this cutting does mean that I no longer have that mass of Ox-Eyed Daisies spreading their bright, white heads all around, though many of them manage to grow, bud and bloom between grass cuttings. When I see big clusters of these plants in the mead-ow, I dig them up and move them up against a boulder, the logs that define the parking area or some other place where the mower will miss them.

Watching the birds splashing and enjoying the birdbath on top of the short log in the salal alcove, I decide they could use a larger dish. I place a shallow 30-cm (12-inch) diameter Mexican pottery dish on top of the log. The Towhees especially, with their flashy rusty-red black and white plumage, love it. So do the robins. They spend several minutes at a time wallowing, fluttering, hopping in and out, splashing, flapping

ROBIN

wings and tails and tossing water in every direction. In hot weather, I refill the dish twice a day.

But one day, the bowl is on the ground, cracked. Doubtless a raccoon has pulled it over. I mend the crack, replace the dish, and drive long nails along the log's upper edge to prevent the dish from tipping over. Two days, later the dish is again overturned, and broken. I buy another dish, this one of a smaller diameter and so less likely to tip. The proportion is not right for the log, but it does stay put.

A few mornings later, I find several rocks from the flower bed borders pulled away and lying on the grass. Dogs? Another flower bed has rocks not only pulled away out of the border but thrown onto the flower bed, crushing a thriving clump of lobelia. This is not the work

RACCOON MOVING ROCKS

BIRDFEEDER
ON TREE STUMP

of a dog. This needed two strong hands, and it has to have been a raccoon in search of the tasty bugs that lie under the rocks. Every now and then I replace overthrown rocks because, short of cementing them together, there is nothing else I can do.

Then the raccoon discovers the bird feeder hanging from a nail driven into the big tree stump in the flower bed near the house. It lifts up the glass sides of the feeder, allowing a large amount of seed—which it loves to eat—to pour into the feeding trough and spill onto the flower bed. I counteract by placing a grooved cross bar inside the feeder to prevent the glass sides from being lifted. That should do it. But the rascally night raider manages to tilt the entire feeder over to one side, letting gravity release a quantity of seed. My solution to that is to drive in 12-cm (6-inch) nails just under the base of the feeder to prevent it from being tipped over. I can almost see this masked bandit thumbing its nose at me with its very dextrous thumb and flexible fingers, which are the source of most of these problems. This has grown into a challenge of wits between us. Now the new trick for the raccoon is to open up the hinged, gabled roof of the feeder. The creature moistens a handlike front paw with its tongue, reaches down behind the glass sides, presses a hand onto the seed, withdraws it, then licks off all the seeds that stuck to it. I haven't seen this happen, but I have been told that this is what they do, and it would account for the rapid loss of seed.

To spoil this little antic, I wire the feeder lid down, but the next night a good upward heave snaps the wire. So then I use a much thicker stronger wire. Perhaps it takes a little more time or ingenuity on the part of the raccoon, but undaunted, those clever, manipulating hands figure out how to undo the wire. I have run out of ideas and am about to give up when two

Vancouver friends, June and Frank Shoemaker, come to visit. Ever resourceful and capable, Frank takes up the raccoon challenge like a crusader takes up his sword. After studying the problem, he visits the island's building supply store and returns with a strong two-part hasp and some screws. Frank attaches one part of the hasp to the feeder's lid and the other to the end wall of the feeder, and I half expect him to produce a combination lock to complete the raccoon-proof feeder fortress. But no, he slips an O-ring through the hasp; and never again does the raccoon raid the bird feeder. It rummages through my compost heap instead.

An evening sometime later, I am hunched in my favourite reading corner. It's late at night and very dark. I hear noises coming from the deck. A prowler? I go over to the glass door that opens onto the deck and turn on an outside light. It's a prowler, all right, and a thief at that. Not 2 m (6 feet) away is a raccoon, crouched under a small table and clutching one of my gardening shoes (the other is still on the doormat). The culprit looks up and stares at me with what I swear is a guilty "caught-in-the-act" expression. I hold its gaze, smiling—amused and happy that the prowler, though masked, is a four-legged one. Slowly, I open the door and the raccoon, still watching me, puts down the shoe, then slowly turns and slips away into the night. Now what would a raccoon want with an old running shoe?

Not long after the shoe incident, I see my prowler friend passing the dining-room windows and realize that it is looking for the dish of bird seed that I sometimes put out in the carport. Out of curiosity, I go to the kitchen window and watch. As soon as the raccoon clambers up onto the woodpile, I am surprised to see it joined by a second raccoon. The two of them fumble around, then stop and look off to their left. I am even more astonished when a third raccoon joins them.

So now I have not one but a pack of raccoons; triple trouble, probably a family. And then I find myself thinking: if I leave food by the deck door, I bet I could tame them in no time. Each evening for five days, I put out pieces of apple or shrivelled grapes, and each morning it's all gone. Twice I see the trio on the deck and we make eye contact through the glass door, which I quietly open. But not yet ready to trust me, they slink away, casually and quietly, beyond the spill of light.

Two days later, I hear the thump of firewood falling from the woodpile onto the carport floor. I flick on the outside light and open the front door. From the edge of the darkness, heads all turned toward me, are FOUR masked raccoons. Well, I only have myself to blame. I head to the kitchen and return with apple slices, wondering how many more of these incorrigible creatures there are out there.

My hanging bird feeder is a continuing source of fascination for me, whatever the season. In the woods, I find a tall bare branch with several side branches and attach it to the tree stump close to the feeder to provide a landing and take-off perch for the birds. The next day, about fifteen Juncos arrive in ones and twos, blowing in from the forest and across the open grass like a burst of autumn leaves in a gust of wind. They settle on the stump, the branches, the flower bed and the grass, taking turns at the feeder, changing places and constantly fighting and flitting around. About the size of a sparrow, the Dark-eyed Junco has a reddish-brown back, slate wings and light undersides; the head and shoulders are hooded in black for the males, grey for the females.

Their boon companions are two, sometimes three, Towhees and a couple of Fox Sparrows. The latter, overall brown and speckle-breasted, are only a little larger than the Juncos. A Towhee, nearly as large as a robin, takes precedence at the feeder. It flaunts its rich, rusty red flanks, which contrast with its white front and black hooded head, while its long, slender black tail keeps up a flickering dance. The Towhee often flits to the ground and disappears beneath the cover of salal, there to spend considerable time scuffling among the layers of dead salal leaves, thick and rot-resistant, in search of bugs and insects. The first time I heard the scuffling, scratching and crashing around, it was so noisy that I thought there must be some animal in the bushes.

A voracious visitor to the feeder is a large, bold, brash bird—beautiful nevertheless. With a strong sense of self, the Steller's Jay barrels its way onto to the roof of the feeder, squawking to announce its arrival, scattering all

STELLER'S JAY

JUNCOS

TOWHEE ON DRIFTWOOD ON TREE STUMP

FOX SPARROW

other birds off in six directions, and taking over. All the foreparts of this jay are a gleaming black, including a head crest which it raises in alarm or fear, giving it a fierce and forbidding look. In bright contrast, the jay's hind parts are a glistening indigo that shimmers richly in sunlight. Sometimes one jay attracts another jay or two. At this point, if I am in the kitchen, I take up a teaspoon and rap it smartly on the window to warn off the jays so the smaller birds can return to feed. But the jays don't stay away for long, so it's rap, fly, rap, fly, until I get tired of rapping and let the birds squawk it out for themselves. Mostly the jays stuff their cheeks with all the small sunflower seeds they can hold, then fly off to stash them away in some secret place I am not allowed to see.

It's a bright sunny morning when a Red Squirrel discovers the bird feeder and becomes a regular visitor, picking out only the sunflower seeds. I name this nervous and frisky little seed-eater "Tamias," a short version of its somewhat lengthy scientific name, *Tamiasciurus hudsonicus lanuginiosis*. It has gleaming reddish-brown fur all over, except for its throat and underbelly, which are white. Its tail is fringed with black. The squirrel makes a distinctive and piercing tzichip-tzichip-tzichip sound—repeatedly, usually from up in a tree somewhere.

Daily, Tamias scuttles head-first down the trunk of a nearby hemlock tree, hastily scuffles its way through the jungle of salal underbrush, and shinnies up the old tree stump that holds the bird feeder. There is never anything casual or unhurried about a squirrel; every move is brisk, positive and deliberate. Even when sitting on a tree branch giving out its tzichip-tzichip-tzichip call, its tail gives a short, sharp flick in unison with each cry. It can, however, freeze without the flicker of a whisker if it thinks any kind of danger lurks.

When I go out on the deck, Tamias vanishes like quicksilver at the sound of the doorknob turning. But gradually, my daily visitor gets accustomed to me, and I can stand on the deck and talk nicely to this squirrel. After a week or so, Tamias lets me go down the steps to the grass before feeling the need to flee. Later on, I am allowed a few steps toward the tree stump and the feeder. Each day, I approach closer and closer, talking softly: "Good morning Tamias . . . Do you like sunflower seeds?" Over time, the distance between us diminishes until Tamias and I are only 60 cm (2 feet) apart. But that distance forms the limit of its tolerance, and any attempt to get closer is too much for the squirrel's instinctive self-preservation. In a flash of fur, Tamias vanishes into the salal.

"TAMIAS"

Birds won't come to the feeder when Tamias is there, so I fill a dish with sunflower seeds for the squirrel and leave it at the base of the stump. Returning the next day, Tamias takes one sunflower seed from the dish, skitters a short way up the stump to a notch and sits there to shell and eat it—then repeats the sequence over and over and over again. Daily. On the fourth day, I count how many times Tamias goes up and down the stump in a single visit. Each complete trip takes eight seconds. I am surprised when the count reaches 50 seeds, amazed when it climbs to 100, and totally astonished to learn that one small squirrel can consume 153 shelled sunflower seeds at a sitting. But probably the squirrel is stashing some of the shelled seeds in its cheek pouches.

Another threat to the bird feeder comes from the island's population of feral cats. Bred in the wilds, they are far more wary than the raccoons or deer, streaking off into the woods in a flash if they so much as hear a doorknob turning. There is a large grey cat that has devised cunning strategies for catching birds around my house. "Greybeard" (as I call it) curls itself up into a tight ball and sits next to a grey stone, of about the same size and shape, beneath the bird feeder. The cat waits, motionless, for a bird to drop down to the flower bed to pick up fallen seeds, then pounces. Small feathers on the soil attest to its success. To prevent, this I enclose the area with a fine black mesh which is hardly visible but blocks the cat's access.

But Greybeard is not stymied for long. In heavy rain or deep snow, I put out a dish of birdseed on the chopping block in the carport, for my sake as much as for the birds. When the seed gets scattered, the birds drop down to the cement floor to get it. One day, I discover Greybeard crouched under the front bumper of my parked car, ready to spring out onto an unwary bird. But to foil that clever tactic, I align three hefty lengths of firewood in a row toward the end of the carport and park with the front bumper right up to the barrier, leaving no room for a predator to hide and pounce.

Whenever I spot a feral cat near the house, I open the door and shout and clap my hands. The cat takes off like a streak and heads for the forest. Then I bark and howl like a dog, to ensure that it keeps on running. I am not a cat hater at all, but these cats are not part of nature's plan; many have been dumped on Quadra by irresponsible pet owners who no longer want them, knowing that the animals will not be able to return home from the island. In time, the wild cats breed and the problems multiply.

To one side of the tree-stump bird feeder, there are two young hemlock trees, which I keep trimming to prevent them from growing too tall and blocking my view from the kitchen windows. In the shade of these trees, I develop a bed of ferns, starting with Deer Fern, which is abundant along Quadra's roadside ditches. These are somewhat similar to sword ferns, but smaller, and with more elegant, slender leaves. I am really fond of ferns and recall that my mother once told me that, in discussing what to name their second daughter (me), she and my father had considered "Bracken," because it would go so nicely with Heather, my sister's name.

To the fern bed I add Spiny Woodfern, a delicate and lacy little plant, then find a place for my favourite: Maidenhair Fern. I love its delicate shade of soft, light green, and the way the leaves grow in a lively swirl on their glistening, ebony stalks. I treasure a small, knob-lidded, spruce root basket made by the Haida weaver Primrose Adams in the Queen Charlotte Islands.

On it is a geometric design woven with the shiny, black stems of Maidenhair. I remember that she said the sharp edges of the stems were hard on her fingers and that she didn't want to use it again—so I bought the basket.

Another fern that I find attractive is Licorice Fern. Its leaves grow singly, cascading down a mossy rock face or from the trunk of a mature tree, often maple. Each leaf springs from the plant's rhizome, which is actually the stem, not a root, growing beneath the moss. This rhizome is quite edible and has a strong licorice taste, which gives the fern its name.

SPINY WOODFERN

My sister, Heather, comes from England for a second visit to Quadra, bringing with her much gardening experience. She has a flower, fruit and vegetable garden greatly enhanced through her many years of creative planting and good care. A bit overwhelmed by my 1.2 ha (3 acres) of meadow and "wild forest," Heather nevertheless enjoys the novelty of it and gives me a hand with the flower beds. But she never quite comes to terms with the idea that deer are free to come and go and help themselves to whatever they consider to be the flavour of the month. If that happens to be a plant listed as being deer-proof, and bought for that reason, well, too bad. Cross it off the list.

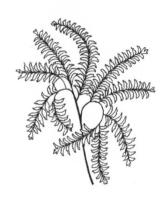

MAIDENHAIR FERN

Heather is also amazed that you can take stones off the beach for your garden. In England, 20-cm (8-inch) stones are sold from big wire bins at garden supply stores, for the

LICORICE FERN

equivalent of about three dollars each. More for larger ones. She would like to take a whole load of them back with her but settles for some attractive pebbles for a friend's fountain.

That summer, Peter and Anne come to stay while Heather is here, and it's a wonderful family reunion, though it lacks their two adult children, Ian and Robyn, who are both away. The following month, Peter and Anne and I join my friends Al and Irene Whitney on their 71-foot sailboat, *Darwin Sound*, for a fabulous week of cruising among the southern Queen Charlotte Islands. Peter delights in taking the helm of this superb vessel and in celebrating his birthday with a candled cake and great joviality—even as he knows he has cancer, and in spite of recent chemotherapy treatment. It is a very special week that I treasure yet.

Chapter 6

Squawks and Screeches

CROW

While I live in the relative peace and quiet befitting a bucolic lifestyle, there are disturbances, sometimes right on my own property. One day, while working around the garden, I become aware of robins screeching with all their might. First a few, and then many, and the commotion continues. Curious, I head toward the source of the racket, which is somewhere within the circular driveway. By now, the sound is shrill, with loud and constant squawking that conveys panic.

Looking up into the trees, I see about fifteen robins surrounding a single crow on a branch. There is no mistaking the robins' fury nor the fear of the crow. Each attempt by the crow to fly off is countered by a flurry of robins preventing its escape. The robins are not attacking the crow—it is much larger—but they are certainly venting their anger and displeasure at the hapless bird, and I suspect that it has been raiding a robin's nest of eggs for a meal. After standing there watching for several minutes, I clap my hands— rightly or wrongly. The intrusive sound scatters all the birds, crow included, and peace reigns again. The robins have shown that there is strength in numbers when a predator shows up.

Not long after that episode, the peace is again shattered, this time by noisome crows, raucous creatures at the best of times. The commotion continues for so long that I finally decide to investigate. The ruckus is coming from the forest on the south side, and I follow a deer trail in. Crows are perched on branches all around the centre of their attention: a young raccoon hunched up on a branch of a large maple. The screeching of the crows is furious and, as before, the object of the birds' anger is too frightened to move. Being good climbers, raccoons can easily access a bird nest to eat the eggs or young, so the mere presence of one is met with aggression on the part of the crows, whether or not a nest is in the vicinity.

..CAUTIOUSLY WALKS DOWN THE BRANCH...

As before, I clap and shout. The crows take off in a flutter of black, leaving the raccoon gathered up into a round hump, looking down at me. I talk softly to it, walking closer, closer. When I pass beneath the branch it is sitting on, the raccoon swivels its head to the other side so as not to lose track of me. I continue speaking gently, sending it good vibrations. Eventually, the masked ball of fur stands up and cautiously walks down the sloping branch, its eyes still on me. I stand very still, excited that perhaps we have each other's trust. When the raccoon reaches the main trunk of the maple, it immediately disappears around to the other side. I hear it scuffle down the

CROWS MOBBING RACCOON

trunk, hit the ground and take off in great haste. So much for trust.

On several subsequent occasions when I hear the scolding and squawking of crows and investigate, I am sure to find them surrounding a raccoon perched on a tree branch, generally with its back to the trunk. One time, from my deck, I watch two cawing crows flap from branch to branch through the woods, probably following a raccoon humping along a deer trail. They just can't help giving raccoons a hard time.

Crows also seem to enjoy harassing ravens. On two occasions, I notice a raven winging its way somewhere, accompanied by two crows flying above, below, or beside it, dipping and rising, and altogether aggravating the raven in its steady flight.

Even more interesting to watch are the manoeuvrable ravens teasing and taunting an eagle. The ravens, in their erratic and flexible flight, have an advantage over the larger, heavier, slower flying bird. The eagle holds calmly to its unhurried flight while the ravens playfully fly over, under and around it, slipping sideways, retreating and returning, swooping and straightening out again.

The raven has to be one of my favourite birds, perhaps because of its strong connection to First Nations culture, in which it is the Creator, and perhaps because of all the many interesting characteristics attributed to it through legend and history. The raven does indeed have a lot of character, some of which even reflects the human disposition, as well as unusual traits quite distinct from other birds.

I first came into contact with these special birds many years ago on camping and exploring trips throughout British Columbia. What I noticed then was the extraordinary sound of the raven's wingbeats, not knowing that it is created by the gaps between the primary feathers at the wingtips. A raven in flight produces a loud swooshing sound that comes in rhythmic spurts with each downbeat of the wings. This can be heard even when a raven is flying at a good height or distance and becomes louder the closer it comes. The raven's call sounds something like that of a crow, except that it is far more fluid, or liquid, and not nearly so raucous. The raven also is capable of making a wide variety of throaty and gurgling sounds with inflections; sometimes words seem to be almost within its reach.

Another characteristic of the raven that I enjoy is its wide repertoire of flight skills, entertaining to watch on a windy day when one of them literally frolics with the wind. Flying straight and level, the bird suddenly flips itself upside-down, flies on, then rights itself again: barrel rolls. Or, with wings held at its side, it drops like a stone, recovers, then swoops upward again. One day, I watch two ravens flying in formation and I can hardly believe their timing and precision. The two fly straight and level, then separate left

RAVEN

and right, turning around and coming back together again, flying almost wingtip to wingtip. Ravens flaunt their aviation skills year round, but more so at mating time, when they mate for life.

Walking back to the house along a wide deer trail, I hear the scolding sound of a Winter Wren. A short distance away to my right, I spot the small brown bird, with uptipped tail, perched on a twig. After chastising me for a minute, it flies right across my path to the broad trunk of an old alder—and simply disappears. It is as though the tree just absorbed the wren. As with many old alders, this one has a cluster of bristling, slender, upright twigs growing from its trunk. There's a small dark oval among the twigs and a closer inspection proves it to be the entrance to a well-disguised, pouchlike nest somewhat unusual for this bird. I add the wren to my list of birds found on my property.

MY CASUAL LISTING OF BIRDS [GULLS NOT INCLUDED]

MONTH			
May	RED SHAFTED FLICKER	JUNE	BLUE HERON - in a tree.
"	RED BREASTED SAPSUCKER	JULY	HAIRY WOODPECKER
"	ROBINS	APRIL	GOLDEN CROWNED SPARROW
"	VIOLET-GREEN SWALLOWS	JUNE	BROWN HEADED COWBIRD
	PILEATED WOODPECKER	JULY	HOUSE FINCH - a pair
SUMMER	EAGLES in maple tree!	NOV	SONG SPARROW
	RAVENS	DEC	SHARP SHINNED HAWK
	RUFOUS HUMMING BIRD		on the deck - window stunned.
	CROWS		
	10 EAGLES - circling high up.	"	PINE SISKINS - a flock
FALL	QUAIL ?	APRIL	WHITE CROWNED SPARROW
	GROUSE - SHARP TAILED	"	STARLINGS
	RUFOUS SIDED TOWHEES	MAY	HERMIT TRUSH - window kill.
DEC	WINTER WREN	OCT	SLATE COLOURED JUNCO
	CHICKADEE, CHESTNUT BACKED	"	RED BREASTED NUTHATCH
	OREGON JUNCOS	JAN	WARBLING VIREO
	STELLERS JAY		
JAN	VARIED THRUSH		
	GOLDEN CROWNED KINGLET		
	BUSH TITS		

NEST of WINTER WREN

WINTER WREN

102

·   ·   ·

Just outside my carport is a row of big sword ferns, planted there to mask the cement foundation of the house. As I am walking by the ferns this day, I hear a loud CHEEP! I stop and look around but can see nothing. Again, a piercing CHEEP. Parting the profusion of long green ferns, I look between the plants. Nothing. Another single and very loud CHEEP, almost a desperate call. I delve more deeply into the bed of ferns while the elusive cheep continues intermittently. The sound is coming from right in front of me, but I cannot find the source. I am baffled but I refuse to give up. Suddenly, I spot a robin, completely upside-down, tail in the air, head and beak right down in the bottom of a clump of ferns. The plant's strong, vertical stems are holding the bird firmly, camouflaging and imprisoning it. Carefully, I slide my fingers down each side of the up-ended bird and lift it out. In a flash, it is gone from my hand, flying across the meadow, seemingly unhurt. I wonder how long it has been in such an undignified position and how it got there. Then I notice there's a window right above the bed of ferns. It seems likely that the robin flew into the window, ricocheted off the glass, and plunged head first into the ferns. Clasped tightly by the stalks, it was unable to free itself.

Some months after the robin incident, I am at home curled in a corner reading. It's almost dark when the peace of the evening is disturbed by a fluttering sound descending in the wall directly behind the wood stove, which is not lit. The chimney stack, enclosed behind the wall, runs from the roof down to the living room and on down into the crawl space beneath the house. A length of stovepipe connects the wood stove to the chimney. I hear more fluttering behind the wall, and I am distressed but puzzled as to what action to take.

All is quiet for a while, until I hear a short burst of fluttering again, then silence. I try to think what I can do, but the continued silence indicates perhaps there is nothing to be done. Was it a crow? A Steller's Jay? I'll have to have the chimney cleaned and have whatever it is removed before I can light the stove again.

Mid-morning the next day, the fluttering is there again, though short and not very vigorous. The sound seems to come from the stovepipe. I would unscrew the screws and pull the stovepipe out, except that (once again) I have one arm in a cast, due to a recent fall and a broken wrist, so that's impossible. I phone Tom Clapham, my regular chimney cleaner and a man with a reputation for his acts of kindness. He says he has to catch the noon ferry, but he'll stop by to see what he can do.

Within minutes, Tom is at my door. He unscrews the pipe, carries it out onto the deck, and shakes it. Nothing. Back indoors, we hear the fluttering coming from further down the chimney, below the opening left by the removed stovepipe. From a bag, Tom takes out a light bulb on the end of an electric cord, plugs it in, puts his arm into the chimney connection, and lowers the light down. Then he holds a mirror over the opening. "It's some kind of a flicker," he says. "Take a look." Squinting into the hole via the mirror, I can see the markings of a Red-shafted Flicker, the bird that drums on my roof, the bird that I have a special fondness for. But HOW to get it out?

As Tom and I discuss the problem, the flicker makes its way back up the chimney, past the open hole. Being a woodpecker, it has feet designed for walking up tree trunks, so it is able to walk up the inside of the chimney. Now what?

Tom asks if I have an old sheet to stuff into the chimney to prevent the bird from going down again past the opening. I find an old tablecloth, which he rolls into a ball. Reaching into the chimney again, he stuffs it into the opening that leads down. "I have to go," Tom says. "If you can make a bag of fish netting or something and put it over the opening, the bird will fly out to the daylight—and you've got him." Arms covered in soot, he races off home to wash, change and catch the ferry.

I am left wondering how to make a bag of fishnet when I have only one functioning hand and no fishnet. There's got to be a way. My brother used to say, "What would you do if your life depended on it?" A bracing challenge. There is a long length of fine netting around the flower bed where the bird feeder hangs, to keep the feral cats from hunting the birds that fly to the ground. But it's far too large to manage with one hand. What else? Ah—there is a short length of the same netting around a young cedar tree in a pot, to keep the deer from browsing it. One-handedly, working slowly, I get the net off the tree, thumbtack it to the wooden trim above the stove, then drape it over the stove and down to the hearth. It's the best I can do. This had better work. If the flicker escapes into the room and flies up into the cathedral ceiling, I will never be able to catch it. No one will.

Now I realize that it's a bit chilly because, without the stovepipe and damper in place, the warm air in the house is being pulled right up the chimney. I fetch a plastic bag and manage to cover the open hole by taping the bag along its top edge only, so the bird can see daylight through the plastic and fly through. The updraft holds the plastic firmly to the chimney, so I am no longer losing heat. I wait. And I wait. I figure the bird must be thirsty amid all the soot; if I place some water there, it might come down. I fill a small dish with water, lift up the plastic flap, and place the dish on top of the old tablecloth, which is blocking the lower end of the stovepipe. I stand to one side so that the flicker will not notice me. Eventually, I see its long, strong beak pecking at the plastic, but the plastic, held firmly by the updraft, just gives slightly. I wait some more. Perhaps I should put some birdseed in there too. With some awkwardness, I manage to lift the plastic flap with a finger and thumb of my good hand, while at the same time clasping a fistful of seed—and suddenly out shoots the flicker. It gets tangled in the netting, flapping, fighting, and frightened. With my one good hand, I try desperately to contain it, knowing that if it escapes I will be living with a loose, sooty bird crashing around the house for days.

In seconds, I lose the battle, and the bird escapes the net. It flies straight for the sunlit forest which it sees ahead through the window, hits the glass, drops to the floor, and scurries to a safe place underneath the settee. Short of staying in the netting, I realize that this is the best thing it could have done. Now I have time to consider my next step. I need a new strategy, and I have a sense this is my last chance, so it had better work. The flicker has a powerful beak, and I can't risk injuring my one good hand, nor do I want it flying around crashing into windows and glass doors.

After thinking the situation through, I devise a plan. Slowly and quietly, I pull the coffee table, which has a solid base, over to one side of the settee. I slide an easy chair over to the same side and move a floor lamp and a plant to the other side. Now there's a clear pathway from the settee to a door that leads to the deck, a distance of about 3 m (10 feet). Taking care not to scare the already panicky bird, I quietly open the door to the deck. The cool air streams in. The bird sees and scents the fresh forest, and in a flash of sooty feathers makes a dash for it, flying straight out the open door and into the bright sun and the safety of the trees. I am relieved and elated—and very appreciative of Tom's kindness.

It's a summer evening and I am just finishing dinner when I see a strange, dark brown bird fluttering straight toward the window. I brace for the sickening thud on the glass, but it suddenly veers away, flops down into the flower bed below the big tree stump, and scuttles under some foliage. That's no bird. It's more like a bat. As I watch, a furry brown body with extended wing membranes hauls itself out onto a flat rock edging the flower bed; then I see that it is a Little Brown Myotis, the smallest of British Columbia's bats at 6 cm (2 1/2 inches). As I stare in amazement, it flies toward the house and out of my sight.

I rush outside and find the bat trying to work its way up between the house's cedar cladding and the cement foundation. Thick festoons of cobwebs hang from under the cedar boards, and as I try to clear these away to make a clean space for the bat, it somehow attaches itself to my finger. The bat keeps opening its tiny mouth, gasping, and I fear it must be close to expiring. I carry it indoors, lay it on the lid of a small cardboard box on the dining table, and offer it a drop of water on the end of a small teaspoon. A tiny pink tongue laps it all up. It drinks most of another drop, then lies still.

Half an hour later, when I return to check on the bat, the cardboard lid is empty. The bat is gone. I look up into the cathedral ceiling and along the beams. No sign of it, but there are many beams and places for it to hide. Eventually, I notice that it is clinging upside-down to the baseboard. Well, of course; it wouldn't be happy lying flat on its stomach any more than I would be hanging upside-down.

By now it is getting on for dusk, and if the bat is going to survive, it should be outside so that it can fly free and feed. I carefully pick it up and again it clings to my finger. I go out onto the deck and transfer "Little Brown" to the cedar framing around the window, hooking its diminutive five-toed feet with their minuscule claws to the top edge so that it is hanging down.

First thing in the morning, I check on my invalid bat, hoping it has recovered and gone. It hasn't. Gently, I run a finger over its back, which is covered with thick fur, golden brown and slightly wavy, to see if it is still alive. "Little Brown" raises its head, with those great long ears, and looks at me. I offer it water again, but it won't drink.

After breakfast, I sit on a cushion on the deck and make drawings of the bat from close range and from various angles. I have been trying to find a photo of the Little Brown Myotis, for the illustrations for this book but have not been successful, as my sources here are limited. This encounter with one is a timely gift that I can hardly believe.

I know that bats like to huddle into corners or small spaces, so I take some pieces of wood from the woodpile and arrange them on top of a bench just below the window. This creates a dark inviting corner, and the next time I look, the bat has moved into its shelter. It stays there all that day and all the next day, though it has now angled itself diagonally.

The bat is still there the following morning, and I make further drawings. As I am about to go indoors, it falls to the deck with a soft plop. Little Brown is dead.

I pick up this extraordinary little mammal and lay it in the palm of my hand. Then I stretch wide the dusky, velvety wings and marvel at the intricate structuring. While the bat's hind legs have feet with tiny, clawed toes, all the same length, four of the five hand digits are enormously elongated. The fifth, the thumb, is very small and ends in a single claw. The four fingers form a framework for the expandable membranous covering. When fully outstretched, these become wings to enable the bat to fly and feed on large quantities of insects, which it finds by echolocation (something like

BAT IN FLIGHT

radar). When not in flight, the bat is able to completely fold up its wings and use its clawed feet to attach itself, head down, to any textured surface. It propels itself forward by using its elbows and feet in a crawling mode. This curious flying mammal, which can live for twenty years, is only one of several species of bats in British Columbia. They are unique creatures which surely deserve our admiration and respect.

Looking back, I realize that I was too engrossed by the timely meeting to consider that I might be bitten, or that perhaps the Little Brown Myotis was sick with, or possibly carrying, rabies.

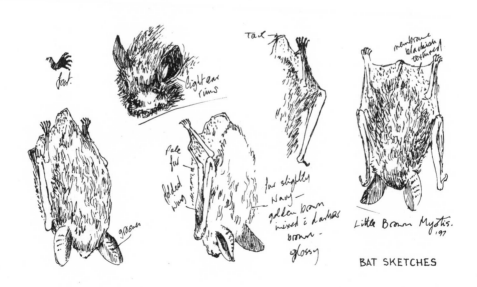

BAT SKETCHES

Chapter 7

Wildflowers and More

I am discovering a rich assortment of wildflowers on Quadra, and hikes with the island's natural history soci-ety provide opportunities to find more. Yet even my own property produces a wide variety over the seasons: in a few years, I count twenty-three kinds. The lupins I seeded years before I moved here form a large purple-blue patch, and the seeds, carried by the wind, are spreading them along the driveway and up the bank. Some are even reaching close to the house. In the fall, I gather their seeds and toss them onto sunny banks along the island's roads.

I do the same with the tall stately foxgloves, which spring up singly or in a mass any place they take a fancy to, as long as it is reasonably sunny. Some foxglove flowers are pure white, some are pinkish, some almost magenta, but all are generous with their seeds. The pods, which are like small closed purses, make them easy to gather. With a plastic bag in one hand, I bend each "purse" over the bag's edge, break-ing the crispy pods to release hundreds and thousands of tiny, tan-coloured seeds. The fox-gloves are perennials, so it will be two years

FOXGLOVE

before they send their long stalks, sometimes head high, soaring up from the big furry leaves at the base. Bees love the foxglove's tubular flowers and crawl deep into them. When I was a kid, I would sometimes pinch the open end of the flower closed with finger and thumb, trapping an unsuspecting bee inside, just to listen to its furious buzzzzzzzzzzz. Then I'd let it out again, hoping it wouldn't turn and sting me in revenge.

I also have big patches of Pearly Everlasting, always so showy in summer with their many-flowered tousled heads gleaming white against the green of salal or other plants. When the flowers are not fully opened, they can be picked and dried by hanging them upside-down on their long stalks. They carry no sweet scent, but in mid-winter they remind me of bright warm days and hold out the promise of another island summer.

One summer, in a potential flower bed in the middle of the meadow, a single columbine appears and flourishes. Soon it is heavy with buds, but a deer devours the prospect of delicate and beautiful flame-orange flowers and goes on its way. The following year, when the plant is well sprouted but not yet budding, I cheat on the deer. I dig up the columbine and put it in a deck tub full of rich soil, and for the rest of the summer enjoy the colourful blossoms dancing on a breezy day.

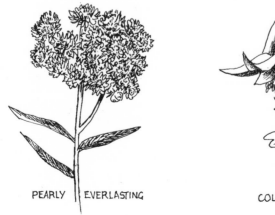

PEARLY EVERLASTING

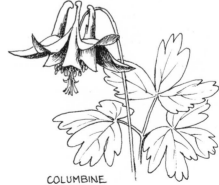

COLUMBINE

110

Looking out my bedroom window, I notice a doe grazing her way across the grass to the flower bed near the house. When she bends her neck to munch a patch of alyssium, I tap on the glass. The deer looks up, surprised, staring at me with those big trusting eyes. Half in jest, and yet with good reason, I wag my finger at the animal, and say, "No! Not my flowers. Leave them alone, please!" As though in resigned obedience, the deer turns her head and walks away. I smile to myself and watch as she crosses the driveway and approaches a slender log barrier, put there to prevent turning cars from running

WILD MINT

over a large patch of young lupins. As the deer takes up that about-to-leap stance in front of the barrier, I rap on the window again. She stops, turns her head and looks at me. "No!" I say firmly. "Go around." Like a creature in a Walt Disney movie, the big-eyed doe goes around the barrier, jumps the ditch and disappears into the forest where no stupid human will dictate what she should or shouldn't do.

...THE DEER LOOKS UP, SURPRISED...

At a summer barbecue with friends at their cabin on Village Bay Lake, I smell the pungent aroma of fresh mint and track it to a large patch at the water's edge. Rising up from the wetland are square stems clasped by pairs of hairy leaves, some with whorled clusters of multiple pink flowers. With permission from the cabin owners, I pick a quantity to take home to dry for tea and for seasoning. As I do so, a couple of Hooded Mergansers paddle by, the male so decoratively pat-

HOODED MERGANSER

terned and coloured it could be an exotic tropical bird.

On another lake, aptly named Mud Lake since most of it consists of just that, are big patches of rich, dark green Tule Reeds. They bend gracefully, casting reflections that look like stringless hunting bows. I have taken a one-day workshop in basketry from Gretchen Peters, learning to weave these dried reeds. Gretchen weaves the reeds into charming wide-brimmed hats which sell in local stores. I gather an armful of the reeds and spread them over my deck to dry in the sun, later making them into a double-sided mat such as the Coast Salish First Nations did. The mat is not really woven but sewn with a long wooden needle I make from a tall, straight stalk of Ocean Spray. The mat and needle were commissioned by an educational institute in Portland, Oregon. Another name for the versatile Ocean Spray is Ironwood, and it lives up to its name, providing ideal barbecue and salmon-roasting sticks because it resists burning. I use lengths of it to support tall garden plants because it also resists rotting and, with its brown bark, the slender sticks are hardly visible. Strong pegs can also be cut from the wood. In summer, island roadsides are thick with Ocean Spray's creamy white flowers in pyramidal clusters, cascading down like ocean waves tumbling and splashing over rocks: hence the name.

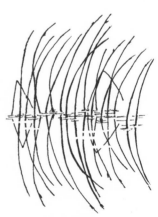

TULE REEDS

More prolific on the island than Ocean Spray is the lavish Scotch Broom. By late May, it splashes the roadsides, meadows and open sunny areas with its brilliant yellow-gold flowers offset by dark green leaves. Whole hillsides turn chrome, waste places become gardens of gold and hedgerows are afire with the blossoming broom, running riot, out of control. Once it gets into in a garden, it is nigh impossible to get rid of. Its peapodlike seed containers explode with a snap in the warm sun, scattering its hard, black seeds, which can lie dormant for up to seven years. Clipping the seedlings only strengthens their growth and root structure. Each new plant must be pulled up by its roots, an endless task.

Another ubiquitous, prolific and fast-growing plant is the Hairy Cat's Ear with its bright yellow dandelionlike flowers on long stems, beloved of the deer. With its head down, a deer will snip off quantities of these flowers as it slowly browses its way across the grass.

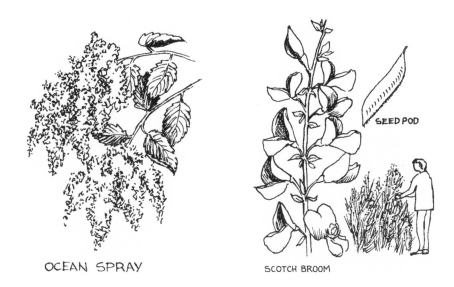

OCEAN SPRAY

SCOTCH BROOM

SEED POD

HAIRY CAT'S EAR

SEED

SWEET-SCENTED
NORTHERN BEDSTRAW

FIREWEED

GOLDENROD

Alongside the driveway, I find a Sweet-scented Northern Bedstraw, with tiny white star-shaped flowers and a swirl of leaves in clusters down the square stems. The plant has many tiny hooked bristles, which makes it cling to socks or any other clothing. When we were kids, we would throw a handful of this long straggly plant onto the back of someone's wool shirt or jacket (no nylon in those days) and giggle as the unsuspecting person (hopefully an adult) walked along in all innocence. Now, it is one of the plants which I use to print designs on hand-made greeting cards.

I notice that wildflowers do not necessarily regrow in the same place every year. The tall, shaggy and showy Canada Goldenrod that grows along the driveway for the first couple of years diminishes, then disappears. The continued growth of overhead alder trees has cut off sufficient sun for these deep yellow spires to thrive. Conversely, new flowers appear where none did before, such as the unexpected gift of the pinky-purple Fireweed, also called Willow Herb. Its seeds were wind-blown, perhaps a good distance, carried by their cotton wool-like pappus, or fluff, to land, germinate and grow at the edge of the meadow. This fluff was once used by various First Nations groups who spun it with mountain goat wool to weave blankets and clothing. They also spun the full grown stem's outer fibre into twine for fish netting and used the plant's young spring shoots as a welcome pot herb.

Another edible plant, excellent in a salad, is Siberian Miners' Lettuce, with its small pinky-white flowers and succulent heart-shaped leaves. I like to add both the leaves and flowers to a salad. The young shoots of early spring salmonberry are another very acceptable salad ingredient, needing only the outer covering peeled off. The best shoots, I find, are those that come up out of the ground rather than from a branch.

I am also keeping a list of the species of trees on my property. Of the conifers, I have Douglas Fir, Balsam Fir and Western Hemlock; in addition, I have planted a White Pine, a Yellow Cedar and a Red Cedar. As for deciduous trees, I have Broad-leafed Maple, Red Alder, Bitter Cherry, Red Elderberry and Mountain Ash. I've also planted an arbutus tree. There are a few magnificent old oak trees on the island (though none on my land), undoubtedly planted long ago by early settlers.

PLANTLIFE ON MY LAND [*incomplete*].
EXCEPTING MOSSES & LICHENS

• INDIGENOUS
✳ INTRODUCED BY ME

TREES	• DOUGLAS FIR • BALSAM FIR • HEMLOCK ✳ SPRUCE	✳ YELLOW CEDAR ✳ RED CEDAR • ELDERBERRY	• MAPLE • ALDER • MOUNTAIN ASH ✳ WHITE PINE	✳ GARY OAK ✳ ARBUTUS	

BERRIES	• SASKATOON BERRY • SALAL BERRY • TRAILING BLACKBERRY • OREGON GRAPE	• SALMONBERRY • FLOWERING CURRENT • HUCKLEBERRY

FLOWERS	• BROOM (TRYING TO ERADICATE!)
	✳ LUPINS
	• FOX GLOVES
	• TRAILING YELLOW VIOLETS
	• COLTSFOOT
	• MINERS' LETTUCE (Siberian)
	• HAIRY CAT'S EAR
	• PEARLY EVERLASTING
	• BLEEDING HEART
	• GOLDEN ROD
	• PIPSISSAWA
	• OX EYE DAISY
	• STAR FLOWER
	• CLOVER - white
	• BALDHIP ROSE
	• SWEET-SCENTED BEDSTRAW
		• DANDELION
		• TWISTED STALK
		• WILD GINGER
		• BUTTERCUP
		• HOP CLOVER
		• HEDGE NETTLE
		• SELF HEAL
		• COLUMBINE
		  YARROW
		• PINEAPPLE WEED
		• SPINEY-LEAVED
		  SOW THISTLE
		• BULL THISTLE
		• BINDWEED
		• FIREWEED
		• KNOTWEED
			MUSHROOMS
			PUFFBALLS
			GEMMED PUFFBALLS
			MEADOW MUSHROOM
			CAULIFLOWER [Fungus]
			BOLETUS (various)
			OYSTER M'ROOM
			UMPHALINA .(umbiella)
			HONEY MUSHROOM
			MOREL
			ORANGE FAIRY-CUP
			BRAIN MUSHROOM
			WITCHES' BUTTER
			STINKHORN

OTHER PLANTS	• VANILLA LEAF • NARROW LEAF PLANTAIN • BROADLEAF PLANTAIN • LARGE LEAVED AVENS • SHEEP SORREL • RATTLESNAKE PLANTAIN • COMMON RUSH • SEDGE	**FERNS** • SWORD FERN • DEERFERN • LADY FERN • SPINEY WOOD FERN • BRACKEN • LICORICE ROOT ✳ MAIDENHAIR FERN

PINEAPPLE WEED

RED ELDERBERRY

116

In late summer, Peter comes to visit me while Anne is attending a workshop in Vancouver, and we spend a special time together. We haul large, sea-smoothed stones from the beach and finish building an embankment along the driveway where the land slopes down toward a ditch. I have a Garry Oak tree, which I grew from an acorn; it's now about 1 m (3 feet) tall and too big for its pot. I choose a place where I would like it to be in the meadow, and Peter replants it, as well as putting up a wire fence to protect it. Deer love Garry Oak.

Peter fixes a cupboard door that doesn't close well and oils the vacuum cleaner. He levels the kitchen stove so that when I break an egg into the frying pan, it no longer slides to the south. After he tunes up my car, we explore more of the island, walking less frequented beaches and coves, bringing back interesting finds, recalling the many camping trips and adventures we shared in our youth.

After a good wind, I can generally find, on the forest floor, twigs with unusual looking lichens growing on them. Some are not the familiar lichens that grow at ground level, and I presume they prefer to inhabit the upper branches of trees. One kind is a clump of flat multibranched prongs, not unlike a reindeer's antler, in a soft grey-green. I spread it out in my flower press—an old Vancouver phone book—under "lic" for lichen and find that it presses and preserves beautifully. I make two greeting cards from it and people ask, "What is it?" When I look it up, I find that its common name is Antlered Perfume. It has no scent, but the name refers to the fact that in ancient times it was used in the making of perfumes; an extract of this lichen helped to maintain the fragrance for many hours. Then I identify another lichen, with frilly, loosely attached leaves of light bluish-green to whitish-grey, as Ragbag. Lichens related to it have, appropriately, common names like Tattered Rag and Laundered Rag. I am very taken by these descriptive names and also thankful that I do not have to memorize names like *Hypoginnia enteromorpha* (Beaded Bone) or other scientific names for the large number of lichens which flourish on this moist coast.

ANTLERED PERFUME

FALSE PIXIE CUP

BEADED BONE

DEVIL'S MATCHSTICK

RAG BAG

I still have the first British Columbia wildflower book I ever bought—fray-edged, loose-spined, corner-worn, thumb-printed and much notated. It is the hardcover, second edition of Chester Lyons's *Trees, Shrubs and Flowers to Know in B.C.* and is even autographed by the author. I bought it in Hope, in the Fraser Canyon, prior to a weekend camping trip with Peter and our companions. The book opened up a new field of my long-standing interest in all growing things, inevitably leading to wild edibles and many other branches of British Columbia natural history. Yet, until this discovery of Antlered Perfume and the Ragbag family, I realize I haven't paid much attention to lichens—and I have been missing a treat.

Walking a trail near Heriot Bay, I pick up a piece of greyish bark. The grey is a crust lichen that completely covers the alder bark, and scattered over it are tiny protrusions in a matching colour. This is Bark Barnacle, and that is just what these fruiting bodies look like: miniature barnacles with a centre opening. My enthusiasm for lichens deepens, and on a trip to Read Island, I find some more: an abundance of Witch's Hair and some Methuselah's Beard, surely the makings for a great Halloween mask with their long wispy strands.

Like miniature, long-stemmed drinking goblets with tiny frayed edges, False Pixie Cups cluster together as though some woodland fairy banquet had just ended. This lichen likes the company of moss and humus in an open shaded site, and bears looking at with a magnifying glass. Almost all the lichens come alive with extraordinary detail when magnified. They leave me marvelling at their complexities of structure, texture and minutiae. So much intriguing beauty so easily passed over.

I find twigs bearing a lichen I identify as Forking Bone, a multilobed, tubular growth, also a soft grey-green. On a tree trunk is its relative, Beaded Bone, similar but jointed like separate beads. I look further. On a rock near a stream, rising from a thin, whitish crust, I discover Devil's Matchstick. The tiny, ghostly stalks, occasionally branched, carry a small black ball-like fruiting body on the tip of each.

I feel that in naming these fungi so colourfully, some botanist has consciously tried to ensure that this lowly form of plant life is not overlooked.

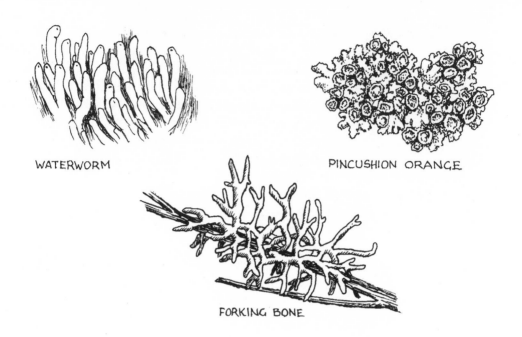

WATERWORM

PINCUSHION ORANGE

FORKING BONE

Then I discover that Trevor Goward, a British Columbia naturalist and liche-nologist, is responsible for many of the whimsical and descriptive names. Thanks, Trevor. To pique the reader's interest, I list a few more names of these humble but fascinating species of fungi:

Punctured Rocktripe, Pencil Script and Peppered Moon; Freckle Pelt and Frog Pelt; Seaside Kidney and Pimpled Kidney; Blood Spattered Beard, Sulphur Stubble and Lettuce Lung.

You could write a poem using these imaginative, tongue-tickling words.

In Any Small Community

I n any small community, public notice boards carry a plethora of signs which reflect something of the area:

the geography, economics, local skills, activities, events and interests. And of course there are the inevitable lost, found and wanted notices.

On Quadra, the major notice boards are in the food stores at both Quathiaski Cove and Heriot Bay, as well as on the ferry. Hand scrawled on a scrap of paper, neatly lettered, typed or computer printed, often with hand-drawn or computerized illustrations, they all have something to say and want to be seen. At times they are pinned one on top of another, two or three deep.

A bold orange sign put up by one store manager declares that all notices must be no larger than 8 x 10 and dated, please, otherwise they will be removed. But a kaleidoscope of papers, all sizes and colours, overlap in fluttering layers like the feathers of a preening duck. Thumbtacks, pins, staples, masking tape and Scotch tape vie with each other to support these offers and gems of island information.

Notices about boats, boating equipment, diving equipment and fishing gear speak of a marine environment. Those about chainsaws, firewood, kindling, wood stoves and livestock indicate a rural area. "Truck for sale," written in pencil on a piece of torn brown paper bag, contrasts with an artist-designed, coloured, computerized poster for a community event. Generally, most of the noncommercial notices are handwritten, though computerisation is on the increase. Names, phone numbers and prices have been omitted from the notices quoted below.

There is a bucolic honesty in these offers:

An enterprising fourteen-year-old with a "Bicycle for transportation" advertises for odd jobs at a reasonable rate, listing various types of work under the heading "I'M GOOD AT:" followed by: "please come to April Point Marina to the sailboat 'Off The Hook' to get a hold of me. Ask for Dan." I do and find him a hard and willing worker.

There's always a wide assortment of items for sale:

For Sale
fResh halibut
at Q. Cove wharf

FOR SALE
NUBIAN GOATS
calves ready for
pasture

FOR SAL
GOOD SOIL CONDITIONER.
AGED SAWDUST and HORSE MANURE
no cedar

FOR SALE · COMPOSTING TOILETS

MATURE ANGORA
GOAT
FREE

In addition to accommodation (which is tight in summer), wanted signs also seek many things:

WANTED
ARICAMA ROOSTER
know where I
might find one ?

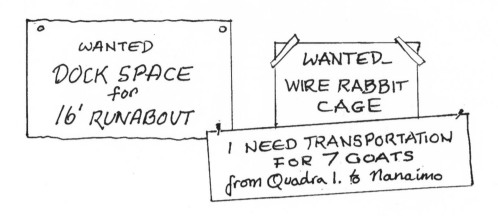

And there is always a sprinkling of lost and founds, especially cats, sometimes dogs, plus other items. A scrawled hand on a scrap of paper announces the following:

LOST.
Husky chainsaw.
Pidcock Rd. bottom of.
on December 2.
fell off truck.

In the cat category,
I have to smile at this one:

MISSING
white male spayed cat,
"LUCY"
Two beautiful blue eyes

One cat notice is on the board for quite a while:

> FOUND: CALICO CAT
> HANGING OUT AT
> QUADRA DAYCARE

Some weeks later, this advertisement appears:

> FREE KITTENS
>
> PART TABBY, PART CALICO

Notice board advertising is both free and entertaining.

When the Red-shafted Flicker starts drumming on my roof on warm spring days, I know it's time to put up my own sign on local notice boards: DRUM UP THE FULL MOON 8 p.m. (and the date) REBECCA SPIT. Each full moon, a bunch of us gather at the spit to drum. We collect driftwood and small logs, light a fire in an iron fireplace above the beach, haul up log butts for circle seating, and warm up our drums by the fire's glow. At first, there are just three or four of us, but others keep drifting in. Some bring not a drum but a percussion instrument like bells, a shaker or bones. One evening, there is a saxophone player who plays with great sensitivity; I am surprised that the combination is so enjoyably compatible. Sometimes beautiful and haunting flute music accompanies the drums as the fire flames dance a fandango. The molten sun loses its grip on the sky and slides down to the mountains, staining the sky and the sea vermilion and gold. People aboard sailboats or power boats anchored in Drew Harbour, having finished dinner and with not a lot to do, row ashore in their dinghies. They and others, out for an evening stroll, sit on the ground or beach logs to watch and listen.

One drummer begins a new beat, and the rest of us pick it up, develop it, enrich it, playing with it until it works itself out and comes to a natural end. An hour or so later, somebody points eastward, proclaiming: "Oh, look—there it is." And rising up behind the mainland mountains is the fat, full moon, the colour of a summer-ripe peach, patterned like an ancient gold coin. The round moon comes up, up, up with the drumming and streaks the water with its spilled reflection. A carpet of warm tangerine light rolls right across the cool, blue-green sea, which is as flat and shiny as a polished marble floor. It is a magic moment. The drumming continues into the evening, resounding across the harbour to the houses opposite. The sound can even be heard on the far side of the island, yet no one ever complains. They enjoy it, they tell us. Around 10:30 we break up and head home, having drummed up the full moon once again.

I have taken several drumming workshops over the years, the first with the Japanese-Canadian drumming group Katari Taiko (the most exciting of all drummers), others with Vancouver's well-known Dido and with Alpha Yaya Dialo, and one with star-status Babatunde Olatunji from New York. I own several different types of drums, but I really covet a *djembe*, a large African drum roughly shaped like a fat-stemmed wineglass without a base, that produces rich, strong sounds. Store-bought djembes I have seen are either not aesthetically pleasing or too expensive. Then in October, I see a sign on a notice board advertising a drum-making workshop on Quadra, all materials supplied. The instructor is Yendor of Cortes Island, whom I have already met through a drumming workshop. Students have the choice of making an *ashiko* (a tall slender cone-shaped drum) or a djembe. I sign up.

There are six participants, and the workshop is held in Anne Lawrence's double carport; she is one of the students. We are each given a large section of freshly cut Yellow Cedar tree trunk, about 48 cm (19 inches) in diameter. The first task is to split off the thick bark with a long chisel and a heavy iron

DRUM MAKING WORKSHOP — REMOVING BARK FROM
YELLOW CEDAR LOG SECTION

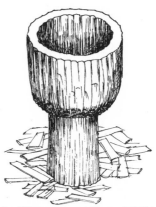

ROUGHED OUT SHAPE OF A DJEMBE.
TOP HOLLOWED OUT.

HOLLOWING OUT COMPLETED

mallet. The ring of metal on metal fills the air while strips of bark fill the carport nearly ankle deep. That day we work from 9:00 A.M. to around 5 P.M., stopping only to eat our bag lunches. The next class is the following week, but there is "homework" to do. The log butt is very heavy; I could get help to lift it into my car to take home, but I couldn't unload it alone, so I leave it at Anne's and return during the week to work on it. The next class, we shape the outside of the log; the third week, we hollow out the inside. All that hollowing and rough shaping supplies me with quantities of kindling. Shaping the

1 2 7

SHAPE FINISHED, SANDED,
BURNISHED AND WAXED

inner curved wall requires a tool called a scaup, and this process produces mountains of wood shavings, most of which go for pathways in Anne's vegetable garden.

Yendor is attentive, cheerful and helpful; he goes from student to student, checking our drums, using specialized implements he has invented to ensure symmetry and an even thickness. He makes and sells drums out of his home for a living; no two are alike, each a work of art. At home, his large coffee table is a huge drum around which several people can gather to play.

Once my drum is hollowed out, it is light enough for me to take home for more work. There are times when my hands and my arms and my back ache all at the same time. After much chiselling, shaping, checking, scauping, sanding, grinding and more, the woodwork is finally finished.

The next week we arrive at Anne's to find five goat hides and one deer hide draped over huge boulders in the garden. We each choose one hide and proceed to scrape the fat off the inner side. It's hard work. We take the hides home to soak in lime and water, then scrape the hair off the skin. Hair gets all over the grass, the flower tubs, the boulders, the wood pile and me.

Next, we make three rings by twisting heavy iron wire into triple circles and cover them with ribbon or whatever decorative material we have brought. I have a piece of cloth that I batiked long ago, and tear it up into long ribbons; the colours are amber, white, grey and a grey-green. Two of the rings hold the hide in place on top of the drum, while the third ring sits well below.

Using quantities of nylon cord, I begin to link the upper and lower rings with vertical stringing. When that's done, the hide (the drumhead) is on firmly, but needs to be tightened. With a special sequence of over and under

SCRAPING GOAT HIDE CLEAN – BOTH SIDES

MAKING 3 IRON RINGS

STRINGING THE DRUM –
WITH GOAT HIDE & RINGS IN PLACE

and back and forth, the horizontal stringing pulls and stretches the hide until it is taut enough to give that distinctive djembe sound.

I burnish the soft cedar wood with a smooth pebble, then polish it with a natural-coloured wax to bring out the richness of the wood and the cedar grain, which swirls around the only knot on the drum, creating a decorative pattern.

To finish off my djembe, I make two lengths of cedar bark twine and glue them into two grooves a few inches apart, near the base of the drum, for decoration. But it needs

FINISHED DJEMBE

something else. Between the rows of twine, I add gleaming white opercula from the Red Turban Snail. Now it is complete. When I play the drum, it sounds good, and I am really proud of it.

I take my djembe to the next full moon drum-up at Rebecca Spit and join a couple of others from the workshop who have also brought their new drums. It's interesting how very different all our djembes are, though we all started out with the same basic block of cedar. We have each put something of ourselves into our drums, and each drum reflects some facet of who we are.

As we continue drumming, I notice a family on the beach just down the bank. A small boy, perhaps five years old, is beating on a drift log with a stick, big eyes watching us, small hand keeping time to our beat. He maintains his participation for quite some time, so I ask him if he would like to join the circle. He leaps to his feet, finds a small log that he can carry, and scrambles up the bank to join us. His name is Christopher, and he is really into it. Soon, another child with a block of wood and stick in hand sits near him, keeping the beat. Then another and another child, boys and girls, all sitting on the grass, concentrating on the beat of their sticks, all keeping the rhythm. Well, most of the time.

After a while, I count nine children of various ages, firelight dancing on their serious faces as they drum along with us. When our drumming comes to a natural break, as it inevitably does from time to time, I suggest that we have a children-only drum session. Little bodies wriggle and wide eyes gleam. "Anybody got a beat?" I ask, not really expecting a response. Christopher's arm shoots up, hand wiggling to catch my attention. "Okay," I say, "what's your rhythm?" After a confused moment, he begins hitting his small log in a one-two-three, one-two-three beat. All the kids join in, beating their makeshift drums with enthusiasm. The dusk of the evening resounds with the clack, clack, clack of wood on wood.

I poke the fire and try to remember when and how I first discovered the power and the joy of drumming.

When 22.7 ha (56 acres) on Morte Lake, on Quadra, are advertised for sale in the newspaper, island resident Linda Van Der Minne happens to notice it. She and her husband, Dirk, get together with Michael Mascal, a dedicated environmentalist, and other environmentally aware islanders. Thus the Quadra Island Conservancy and Stewardship Society is born to purchase the land. Private development would put an end to the pristine quality of the lovely lake and deny public access to its sandy beach, swimming holes, fishing spots and an area of beautiful forest. There is strong community support to save and protect this special place, even though logging is a threat in the foreseeable future. Through the tremendous effort and generosity of many people who make interest-free or minimal-interest loans, and other fundraising, the money for the down payment on the property is raised by the deadline and the lake is saved.

I find myself on the conservancy committee, and for the next three years we organize a broad spectrum of fund-raising events, from annual garden tours to a major auction that includes works by Bill Reid, Robert Davidson, Roy Vickers, Robert Bateman and a Jack Shadbolt exhibition poster, some donated by the artists. The auction raises over $17,000. Eventually, the mortgage is paid off and so are the loans. The mortgage-burning celebration draws a huge crowd and is the biggest potluck supper the Community Centre has ever seen. Now this big tract of lakefront property belongs to all islanders forever more.

Not long afterward, a committee of the Mitlenatch Field Naturalists Society on Quadra produces a natural history guide to the Morte Lake Trail, which is given away to hikers. The twelve-page booklet is researched and written by Steve Mooney, and I do the illustrations and layout. The guide includes some of the particularly interesting flora and fauna of the area.

Here are some excerpts with illustrations and abbreviated text:

"A large shrub with peeling bark called Ninebark. You can probably count more than nine layers of shredding bark on this one, as it is particularly large. This damp-ground loving shrub can also be recognized by its three-lobed leaves and its clusters of white balls of flowers in May–June, or later the reddish clusters of seed capsules."

"Small holes dug in the moss are made by Northern Flying Squirrels during their nightly truffle hunts. The fragrant underground truffles make up a large percentage of this squirrel's diet."

Flying Squirrel

"Western Hemlocks . . . the small needled evergreens with the drooping tips . . . gnarled, deformed branches indicate an attack by the Hemlock Dwarf Mistletoe, which is a parasitic plant that penetrates the tissue of the hemlock and lives within the tree . . . This mistletoe appears as a scaly, olive-green twig with swollen berry-like-fruit sticking up from the branch."

Mistletoe

"The rare Gnome Plant . . . is a fragile cluster of salmon pink flowers with yellow centers growing through the moss like a small wedding bouquet. This plant has no chlorophyll and derives its nutrients from a relationship with fungi."

Gnome Plant

"A tiny red coloured plant—the Round-leaved

Round-leaved Sundew

Sundew . . . is able to survive on poor soil by trapping small insects on the sticky hairs of its glistening, enzyme laden leaves and then slowly digesting them. "

Wolf and scat

" On a winter evening you may be lucky enough to hear wolves singing on Beech's mountain high above the lake. Wolf scat (feces), full of deer bone and hair, is regularly found along the trail. "

You know it's spring when the island's Saturday farmers' market starts up. Stalls and tables line the rim of the newly cut grassy meadow at Quathiaski Cove. Some sellers are there every week, setting up on the shady treed side or on the open sunny side.

You know it's spring when tables are piled with green and growing things and when customers head back to their vehicles, carrying armloads of young plants to grow: flowers, vegetables, herbs, shrubs and even small trees.

As spring turns to summer, sellers offer a variety of tender, organically grown baby vegetables. You know it's summer when you can buy fresh home-grown fruit and pies made from them. Home-baked goods are always popular, from loaves of exotic bread to cookies made by the little girl who is selling them.

One man is offering Shitake Mushrooms, which he raises himself. A small log serves to display the delectable, stemmed fungi, each looking like a small brown saucer attached to the log's bark by its own bracket. Another man offers fruit popsicles, which are often made from wild berries.

Crafts abound as they do on any island: lapidary items; jewellery made from silver, feathers, copper, wood, glass and shell; hand-painted sweatshirts and T-shirts; stained-glass that sparkles in the sun; soft cushions and cuddly teddy bears. There's original art on display, too, and the skilled work of potters' hands. Woodworkers offer toys and bird feeders as well as fine garden furniture of cedar salvaged from the beaches or made from driftwood.

You know it is truly fall when the air cools, falling leaves drift down onto the grassy meadow in the Cove on a Saturday morning—and no one is there.

Chapter 9

Summer and Fall Pickings

SALAL BERRIES

Summer into fall is berry-picking and jam-making time. Those with established gardens gather and preserve all manner of fruits and vegetables, filling shelf after shelf with the generous bounty of nature and sharing it with friends. From Hilda, the gift of a jar of her own quince jelly; from Shirley, a jar of raspberry jam; and from Dennis, my invaluable car mechanic, home-grown kiwi jam made by his wife, Daphne.

Though I am envious of these accomplishments, I turn to my own prop-

EATING SALAL BERRIES

erty and pick several pounds of delicious ripe salal berries. The deer relish these superior berries too, and because I feel an obligation to share the bounty with them, we have a pact. I will pick berries only from chest height and up, and the deer will take all they wish from the same level down. It works just fine. They manage to weave their way right into the thick mass of salal shrubs, often with only their heads showing or just two large ears, feasting on the plump juicy berries until no ripe ones are left. In a few days, when more have ripened, the deer will be back—as will I. Surprisingly, many people think that the purplish-black salal berries are poisonous, even some people who hike and frequent the outdoors. The only snag is that the juice tends to stain the teeth, but it is temporary and the jam is worth it. I often give a jar to visiting friends. Here's my recipe:

Wash the berries and remove bits of stalk, leaves, etc. Mash the berries and, without adding water, simmer very slowly until the mixture bubbles. Add sugar to taste and a splash of vanilla or almond extract for that extra delectable flavour. Seal with wax, or freeze. Wonderful in tarts, squares or with ice cream.

Also on my property I have one tall, sprawling Saskatoon Berry bush, but I have never been able to harvest the fruit as flocks of robins take over in a constant flutter and always beat me to it. Nor have I been able to make a pact with them, so it's all theirs. But I know of a bank massed with Oregon Grape and simply can't help picking enough for at least a couple of jars of tangy jelly. Fiercely bitter, these berries, with their soft blue bloom and hollylike leaves, need a lot of sugar—be warned. Salmonberries and thimbleberries are best eaten fresh.

SASKATOON BERRY

OREGON GRAPE

SALMONBERRY

THIMBLEBERRY

HUCKLEBERRY on STUMP

HUCKLEBERRY

Quadra abounds in huckleberry bushes. Many roadsides are thick with the delicately leaved, square-stemmed plants, lovers of moist places and rich acidic soil. The berries, small and brightly orange, have a refreshing tartness to them. A large fishing resort on the island buys them from pickers and uses them in ice cream. Many an old tree stump sports a huckleberry bush growing like a shaggy, unkempt wig atop its head. Over the years, the wood on the top of the stump breaks down and rots, and from this springs thick moss with lichens growing down the bark. Huckleberry seeds, carried by birds, germinate in the rich humus and the moss; sometimes salal joins with huckleberry and other plant life to form a miniature garden on the stump top. Insects like to make their home in the old stumps; woodpeckers can hear their movement and vigorously peck away at the old wood, often ripping off sizable chunks or making deep holes. Over time, the stumps decay, rot, and fall apart, returning to the earth to enrich the soil for other plants.

•   •   •

Spring to fall in the forest is the time of abundance for exotic, delicious—and valuable—mushrooms. The decaying loam and rich, raw humus of the moist rain coast forest smells pungent and exquisite, an aroma well suited to the many fungi that make a sudden appearance—followed, frequently, by a hasty departure when serious pickers are abroad. They know the best places to go, usually a considerable hike from the road, and spend long hours searching for and picking mushrooms to sell. Cars parked along the gravel roads that wind through the deep, silent forests are often a sign that mushroom pickers are at work.

Rains in September and October bring out the Chanterelles, which range in colour from yellow to almost saffron and orange. These mushrooms are really delicious and sought after. Driving along, I spot a bold hand-lettered sign on a telephone pole announcing MUSHROOM BUYER and follow the pointing arrow. Further along the road is another sign, this one with a drawing of a mushroom, and parked vehicles. I am at Wayne Assal's buying station. Trestle tables in front of the house are roofed over against the rain, and on them are high stacks of dozens of open-work plastic baskets full of Chanterelles. Wayne is busy buying from pickers, but during a lull he tells me that the lidded plastic baskets, called cases, each hold

CHANTERELLE 7·5 cm [3"]

PINE MUSHROOMS. UP TO 20cm [8"]

up to 7 pounds of mushrooms; a five-gallon bucket holds 25 pounds. (Wayne doesn't use metric and neither do the pickers.) He says that on a good day a hard-working picker can bring in a hundred pounds. He also tells me that, though it takes a little longer, mushrooms should be cut and not pulled up, as this destroys the mycelia, a threadlike strand something like a root.

Pickers from Read Island as well as Quadra bring in the results of damp, back-breaking work, and are paid by the pound according to current rates. If there have been heavy rains for a while, the mushroom buyers close down, as too much rain causes mushrooms to take up an excess of water that makes them soggy and undesirable for eating.

Well into October, or until it turns cold, another gourmet mushroom that is even more valuable becomes the prize species. Called a Pine Mushroom because it is often found under pine trees, it can command a very high price depending on condition. A #1 specimen, Wayne tells me, is white, mottled with cinnamon and has an unbroken veil. A small break in the veil drops it into the #2 category. Five categories define the value of this mushroom, which can take on a variety of shapes.

At one time, a lot of mushrooms went for canning, but not any more. At the end of each day, Wayne takes the mushrooms over on the ferry to Campbell River, to be flown to Vancouver and then overseas to please the palates of wealthy gourmands. The Chanterelles go to Europe and the Pines go to Japan, where they sell for outrageously high prices.

Another delicious mushroom is the Morel. It has a strange, convoluted and pitted appearance, as though a cone-shaped, fine wire mesh had been dipped in melted chocolate—plain and milk —and set on a stalk. A picker needs sharp eyes to find these because they blend so well with the forest floor. There is also the weird-looking, dark brown False Morel, also called Brain mushroom for obvious reasons.

There are many less exotic but tasty mushrooms. One autumn, the edge of my driveway sprouts a generous crop of Gemmed Puffballs; as fast as I pick them, up come replacements in a never-ending stream. I enjoy many a

MOREL 6cm [2½"]

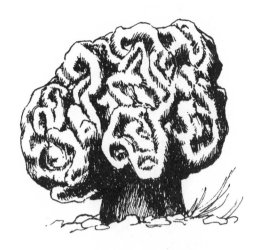

FALSE MOREL or BRAIN MUSHROOM
10cm [4"] WIDE

GEMMED PUFF BALLS _ to 3.2cm [1½"]

SHAGGY MANE _ to 12cm [5"]

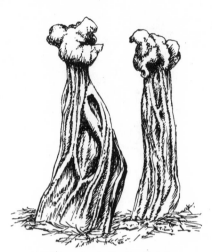

STINKHORN. 6cm.[2½"]   ELF'S SADDLE. 7cm [3¼"]

breakfast of fried egg and sliced puffballs, until the slugs find them. But then I also have plenty of plain puffballs, which pop up in the meadow after rain.

Another mushroom, one of my favourites for eating, is the easily identified Shaggy Mane. These grow clustered together—a few or a large patch—and can push up through extremely hard surfaces, even hardtop. As they mature, the colour changes from white to a partial tan, and they develop the upturned scales that give it a shaggy look, hence the name.

A strange mushroom I have long read about but never seen appears on my property after a rainy spring day. Standing in the bright viridian grass near the house is a solitary Stinkhorn. The top of its tall, pinkish-orange hollow stem has a glob of a slimy, greenish-black mudlike substance that carries the spores. In addition to being somewhat unattractive, the Stinkhorn has a strong and foul odour, perhaps to attract the insects which distribute its spores. The Stinkhorn originates within a round ball, much like a puffball, but with a thin skin. As the spongelike stem of the mushroom grows, it breaks through its skin, rising up in all its bizarre glory. Stinkhorns are generally found in groups, but mine is solitary—and I think perhaps one is all I need.

Also in the never-seen-it-before category is a whimsically shaped mushroom commonly called Elf's Saddle, a (sometimes) descriptive name. Walking at Rebecca Spit after a lot of mild autumn rain, I spot first one, then another, then whole clusters of Elf's Saddle that look like something from a fantastical illustration for a book of fairy tales. Varying considerably in shape from one another, their caps are greyish to black atop an erratic white stem.

While walking down my driveway on a fall morning, looking all around as usual, I notice something white in the woods and go over to investigate. It turns out to be a large, creamy white Cauliflower Fungus. Typically, this

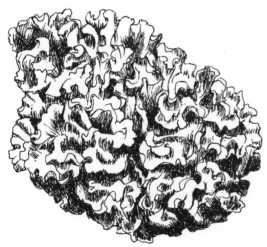

CAULIFLOWER FUNGUS 21cm [8¼"]

BIRD'S NEST FUNGUS 13mm [½"+]

strange-looking, frilled fungus grows on a rotted hemlock root. I fetch a knife and slice it off at the base. It's so big that, out of curiosity, I take it over to the food store to weigh it: exactly 906 grams (2 pounds). After giving away some big chunks of this edible fungus, I break up the rest and dry the pieces in a very slow oven. When the bits are crispy dry, I crush them to a coarse powder and store it in a jar for use in soups and stews to add a strong, rich mushroomy flavour. Because Cauliflower Fungus tends to get tough when cooked, I feel nature intended it for this higher purpose.

Not a mushroom is a quite small but intriguing fungus commonly called, with good reason, Bird's Nest Fungus. Only about 6 mm (1/2 inch) across, it is shaped much like a bird's nest, round and hollow. To add to the similarity, there are several spore-bearing "eggs," whitish and roughly oval, nestled together inside. I have known about this fungus for many years, but only through photos in my mushroom identification book, so I am thrilled to find a cluster of them on a piece of rotting wood. Nature has endowed this rather odd little creation with an enchanting and unusual method of dispersing its spores. When a drop of rain falls directly into the "nest," it splashes one of the "eggs" (each containing a large number of spores) over the rim and out. How long did it take evolution to figure that one out, I wonder.

A new hiking trail has been opened along the east side of Quadra north of Heriot Bay, part of it along the rugged coastline. Steve Mooney offers to show it to me, and on a mild September afternoon, I rendezvous with him. His wife, Anita, can't join us today, but he brings their four-year-old twins, Seamus and Gina, who are already seasoned hikers. I join them in their four-wheel drive, and we travel some distance through a woodlot. Woodlots of up to 400 ha (988 acres) are available to individuals under a fifteen-year licence that is renewable every five years. The licensee manages the woodlot on a long-term basis for sustained yield and biodiversity, harvesting selected trees, planting new ones, and encouraging natural regrowth. This type of logging has a minimal effect on the environment, so that the woods remain attractive to both wildlife and hikers. This particular woodlot has been managed for over twenty years.

After reaching the start of the trail, we park and walk downhill through maple, fir, alder and cedar trees. Young Seamus identifies a Russula Mushroom with its red top, and I find a cluster of mushrooms which I can't name. Steve says they are *Stobilurus trullisatus*, which like to grow on old cones. "I bet it's a fir," he says, pushing four fingers into the moist loam. He brings up a fir cone bearing the fungus, then puts it back. Further down the trail, Seamus points to some small mushrooms on a log, declaring, "These are Golden Trumpets." Steve takes a look and agrees with him, but I am doubtful. When the youngster goes ahead, I ask Steve. "No," he says, smiling, "but I didn't want to discourage him."

The trail goes down to a small bay, sheer rock on one side and a log-strewn beach on the other. Across the water is Read Island, with the mainland mountains beyond. Continuing on the trail, we walk along the ragged, granite coastline edged on the other side by a wall of dense forest and salal. At intervals, stone cairns along the open rock signal to hikers that this is indeed the trail. The children refer to the cairns as "schwegillins," a word that their father made up and which they delight in saying. Frequently, they pick up or point to things and ask questions, alert and interested in their outdoor world.

"There's a loon," says Steve, setting up his spotting scope on a tripod to look out over the grey sea. "And a Bonaparte Gull," he says, adding, a moment later: "Oh, and an Oyster Catcher and Turnstones." His vision is extraordinary. As we clamber up and down rock ledges, the twins sure-footed and confident, I find the last few stragglers of Gumweed, bright yellow among the dead ones. Gina finds Harebells and Hairy Cat's Ear. Steve tells me

OYSTER CATCHER

THRIFT or SEA PINK

MONKEY FLOWER

COMMON RED PAINTBRUSH

CHOCOLATE LILY

that in late May, the fissures in the rock support a profusion of other flowers: Blue-eyed Mary, Sea Pink, Monkey Flower, Common Red Paintbrush, Aqualegia, Nodding Onion and Chocolate Lily.

We reach a high flat area, largely covered with moss and supporting several wind-twisted Shore Pines. A shallow pond of fresh water reflects the pines, and a tiny-leafed plant glistens at the edge. "Sea Milkwort," Steve says, "it's edible." And he should know; he once spent four months paddling a canoe from Vancouver to Quadra, living on wild edibles and fish he caught. I don't know this plant, so I give it a nibble and find it's quite tasty. Steve warns me that it must be cooked before eating to avoid ill effects. Meanwhile, his sharp eyes scanning the water, he announces, "Oh, a Rhinoceros Auklet—and Harbour Seals on Hoskyn's Rock, lots of them." He focusses the spotting scope and invites me to take a look. Way in the distance, on a large outcrop of rock off Read Island, about thirty seals are hauled out sunning themselves.

HARBOUR SEALS HAULED OUT

We climb down giant rock steps and past another schwegillin, with Steve constantly checking land and sea, near and far. He spots a Horned Grebe out on the water, then a Glaucous-winged Gull eating an Ochre Starfish. I never knew a gull could do such a thing. Through the scope, I observe the gull, head set back awkwardly on its shoulders and cheeks filled out; sticking out from its beak are three legs of the hapless starfish. The bird is slowly digesting the other two legs. Steve remarks that there is not a whole lot of nutrition in such a meal, but the gull will get some protein from it.

Next we come to another bay and scramble over a solid mass of windblown logs, including an upended tree stump with a huge arched and twisted root system. The twins immediately wind themselves in and around and through the contorted structure of this natural jungle gym. Hiking onward, we hear a Winter Wren, and Steve imitates the call of a Pygmy Owl to scare it up so that we can see it. He says that all small birds react to this sound by flocking together for safety, but this one must be a loner as nothing appears.

At the next high point, we decide to turn back. When we reach the first bay, Seamus runs ahead to the beach and calls for us to come and see what he has found. Between logs above the high-tide line is the well-aged carcass of a deer. And there is more to come. On the far side of the beach, at the

PURPLE OR OCHRE STARFISH

HORNED GREBE.

GULL DIGESTING OCHRE STARFISH

GINA & SEAMUS AMID DRIFTWOOD

water's edge, is a dead and decomposing wolf. A large, decaying hole in its side, together with broken ribs, strongly suggest it was shot. This area is known to be frequented by wolves, Steve tells me; tracks have been sighted and there is a den in the vicinity. He believes that finding the two dead animals in the same bay is more than a coincidence; in all probability, the wolf, feeding on or drawn to the deer carcass, was shot by a hunter, too many of whom despise wolves.

We are saddened that this large and impressive creature should have been deprived of its life in this senseless way. In silence, we return to the truck.

·   ·   ·

Around fall and into winter of each year, I discover that the lower branches of young trees have been trashed, but I never see who or what is responsible. Broken branches hang down from the trees or lie on the ground, and the outer bark of tree trunks is often shredded or damaged. A Yellow Cedar that I planted on the edge of the forest, even before I moved to Quadra, bears the scars of having its bark shredded when it was young. The cedar, which prefers to grow at high elevations, came to me via a hiking friend who got it as a seedling from the road's edge on a hike up Mount Washington on Vancouver Island. Some other young conifers, which I transplanted to the meadow and are now several years old, suffer the same damage. Even the branches of a Nootka Rose are broken right off. I learn that the culprits are deer—bucks, to be precise—and that the practice is called "fraying." The bucks rub off the velvet from their antlers and also rub the scent glands on their head against the trunks of young trees, trashing the lower branches in the process, in order to mark out their territory. They seldom do this on older trees with sturdy trunks. Steve Mooney believes that the bucks are also sparring with the springy branches and flexible trunks of young trees in mock fights, practising doing battle with rival males and showing off their strength. To prevent this damage until the tree trunks are stronger, I wrap them in tough cord netting, but the bucks still go after the flexible branches as far up as they can reach.

TREE TRUNK HEAVILY
FRAYED BY DEER

Deer don't mind the rain at all. I watch one of them saunter across the meadow in a downpour as happily as though it were a bright summer day. Then, it casually folds its legs and sits down in the middle of the meadow, chewing its cud for at least twenty minutes. (Like cows, deer are able to regurgitate the food they swallow and rechew it to extract further nutrition from the fodder.) When a deer's fur becomes heavy with rain, the animal simply shakes vigorously like a dog after a swim. I have followed deer trails through the forest and found their dens—flattened areas up against a log or beneath a cluster of old conifers—but I have never come across young fawns in the spring. For several weeks, the mother leaves her young when she goes foraging, and the fawns know they must stay hidden. Later, they emerge to be weaned and to browse, frolicking and exercising their legs to strengthen them.

One day, I look out the window and see a doe licking her fawn—its face, its neck, its back. Then the little one begins licking its mother at the same time. Are they bonding? Is it for the pleasure of the physical contact? I am not sure, but it is touching to witness this tender scene being played out so close to my windows—and I forget to fetch my camera.

When the pair return to grazing the grass, I take two apples and walk out onto the deck. The doe and fawn look up at my presence, standing motionless, eyes fixed on me. I throw the apples toward them, hoping the gesture won't appear threatening and frighten them off. When the apples stop rolling, the two of them break their freeze and go for the apples, munching on the treats. This reminds me that it is time to gather up windfalls from the orchards of friends to feed the deer. I scatter the fruit by their trails because deer need to fatten up to face the winter ahead when there is much less for them to eat. A tough winter can be hard on them; a lack of nutritional food causes hair loss and large bald patches on their bodies.

YOUNG BUCK IN THE RAIN, CHEWING CUD

I head across the road to my good friends and neighbours, the Tyes. They provide me not only with windfalls but let me pick small apples (still on the trees) that show little promise of fulfilling their potential this season. Sometimes, if I arrive early for the ferry, I walk down a trail that straggles along the cove and behind the netlofts to pick up a few apples from a tree close to the beach. Unpruned for many years, or maybe never, the tree bears fruit of no great size or quality, but fine for the deer.

Now that I've gathered apples, I head to my favourite blackberry patch, taking with me a long stick with a hook at the end to help bring the tall stems full of ripe berries within reach. But by now the berries are pretty much picked over, so I

DOE WITH FAWN

decide to return in a few days when more have had a chance to ripen. Further along the path, I notice a sprinkling of small, round plums from an old tree gone wild. The orangey-red fruit is scattered over the ground, like big shiny marbles. Using my blackberrying stick, I reach up to shake the fruit-laden branches and am rewarded with a shower of ripe plums all around me. I gather them up and take them home. If the deer don't like them, the raccoons will. Turns out the deer do like them.

It is September again, the grass no longer needs cutting, the woodshed is full, the tourist booth closes, the Saturday farmers' market ends and Quadra Island looks inward once more. I start to walk along the deck, but my way is barred by a huge spider web with long anchoring strands that run from the roof edge to plants in a tub and elsewhere. Suspended in the centre is a perfectly crafted work of art. Sunlight emphasizes each dew-covered gossamer strand of this intricate web, turning them into strings of tiny opalescent beads gleaming against the dark of the forest. How perfect the arrangement, and how functional. What part of a spider's brain, I wonder, holds the knowledge of how to spin this marvel of construction? Later in the morning, there is a hole between the delicate strands, made perhaps by some struggling insect. Watching the spider repair the hole reminds me of how I used to darn the holes in my socks when I was at boarding school. But the spider is far more adept than I was. I also recall that I used to catch some small insect, throw it onto a spider web and watch, fascinated, as the spider, alerted by the vibrations, came rushing down. With its legs, the spider quickly spun the insect around and around as though it were on a spit, at the same time wrapping it up with a strand of web extruded from its body. The poor victim became quite immobile. Later, the spider would make a meal of the soft parts. I am tempted to toss in an insect once again—but I resist.

The deck seems to be a good source of a variety of bugs— especially beetles. One is all black, with two bright red stripes on its head; another is grey, beautifully patterned in black and quite large, while yet another is black and yellow. There is also a hairy legged spider, its back rimmed in reddish-orange, which I haven't seen before. I never saw any of these insects in my Vancouver garden. Steve is away, so for identification I turn to Alana Mascali, who used to work in the entomology department of the American Museum of Natural History in New York; her personal library is extensive, and she is always willing to share it with me.

From one of her books, I identify the grey and black patterned beetle as a Western Pine Borer. The only pines on my property are two small White

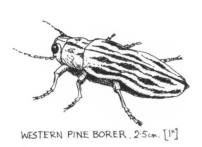

WESTERN PINE BORER. 2·5 cm. [1"]

BURYING BEETLE 1·8 cm [¾"]

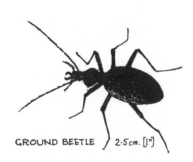

GROUND BEETLE 2·5 cm. [1"]

JUMPING SPIDER. 8 mm. [5⁄16"]

FIREFLY. 1·5 cm. [9⁄16"]

153

Pines that I planted in a flower bed to grow against the house (until they grow too large), so I am not too worried unless the beetle's arboreal tastes are more extensive. I also identify the black beetle with the yellow patterns on its back as a Burying Beetle. It has the interesting habit of rolling over and buzzing like a bee when disturbed—which it does when I pick up a dead and decaying Pine Siskin from behind a planter, and find the beetle. Had the dead bird not been on the wood of the deck, the beetle (and its mate, which is not present) would have removed the earth from underneath it, mated, and laid eggs in the hollow. The larvae would hatch, feed on the carcass, enter a dormant state (pupate), and eventually emerge as beetles.

A beetle with a red rim around its head, much like a Roman arch, is not in Alana's book, but Steve identifies it for me. It is a species of firefly. "But this type doesn't glow," Steve says, adding, with a smile, "the rain has put out its fire." And there is the often-seen ground beetle which digs into the ground for its food.

The small, orange-rimmed spider with fuzzy legs and four white dots on its back, Steve identifies as one of the jumping spiders, so called for their hunting technique. The spider has eight eyes arranged in three rows, giving it exceptional peripheral vision. When the spider sees an insect move, it jumps suddenly onto the unsuspecting prey, which doesn't stand a chance.

Underneath any rock I know I will find a sizable population of soft-bodied Wood Louse, also called Sowbugs, grey and looking like tiny armadillos; they scramble off in all directions when disturbed. Similar to these are Pill Bugs, hard-backed with a series of segmented platelets; when touched, they roll up into a completely round ball and stay that way until all danger has passed.

As September turns into October, the enormous, multitrunked, Broadleafed Maple on the edge of the driveway drops its big ten-pointed leaves, covering the earth as far as it can reach with a rich counterpane of chimneybrick red, apricot and yellow. The tall maple toward the west side of the meadow does the same. Alders don't have that aesthetic sense of beauty nor

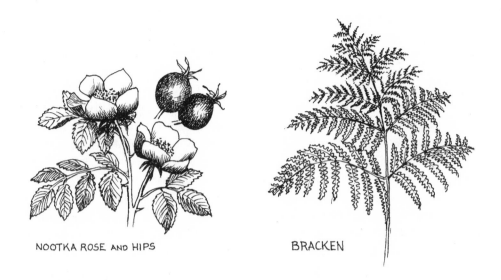

NOOTKA ROSE AND HIPS

BRACKEN

a desire to go out in a blaze of glory; they just drop their leaves—still green. The Nootka Rose flaunts its orangey-red, pear-shaped hips, warm and vivid against the chill morning sky. Towering over some evergreen salal patches are the huge umbrellalike Bracken Ferns, turned to a rusted-iron colour. The very last of the salal berries are still hanging on the bushes, and the deer work their slender bodies in among the thick branches, making inroads to reach the last of the tasty black fruit. This year, I didn't have time to pick salal berries and make jam, and I promise myself that next year I will.

There is always next year. Or is there? On October 24, my beloved brother succumbs to his illness; and though I am deeply grieved, I acknowledge and treasure all that we have shared since childhood. Instead of a dreary funeral, Anne creates a vibrant and beautiful CELEBRATION OF PETER'S LIFE at their home in Vernon. People come from all over to express their appreciation and to share their memories of this special person: his playful sense of fun and adventure, his creativity, his ingenuity, his kindness and caring. There are so many wonderful and touching memories recalled.

Although I have added two more flower beds to the southwest side of the house, the side that faces the wide open meadow still looks rather uninteresting. The small oak tree and the Mountain Ash that I planted will need several more years to really establish their presence. I need to break up the long slope down from the house, northward, so I dig up two small fir trees from the edge of the forest; to decide the best place to plant them to form a foreground interest to the house, I walk up the driveway as well as check from inside the house. But the two firs are still not enough. I come to the conclusion that a terrace, edged by boulders, would relieve the characterless slope. I put the word out that I am looking for a lot of boulders of varying sizes. I check with excavators. I go to two construction sites.

Eventually, I connect with Matt Martinelli, who cleared part of his land to plant a vegetable garden and was left with a big pile of rocks, all sizes. He'd be very happy to have them hauled away. Perfect. I go to check out the boulders and find the pile covered with sprawling blackberry vines, but what I can see of the rocks looks promising. I phone Doug Peters, and he loads up every last rock from Matt's place and dumps them all beside my driveway.

My plan is to form the terrace in a rough S-shape, with the largest boulders at the highest point of the terrace embankment, tapering off to smaller ones up the slope. I choose which rocks should go where, and like someone using chopsticks, Doug works his excavator with its hydraulic thumb to carefully pick up and position each boulder just where I want it. If I change my mind, he patiently moves the rock again.

One particular boulder is quite different from the others, and I can't find a place for it along the terrace edge. When eventually the boulders are all in place, I am left with a pile of small rocks and this large, singular stone, which is about 1 m (40 inches) or more tall, and more or less oval. The silicate sandstone is streaked and has a distinct sparkle. This rock is different and has character. Suddenly, I know what to do with it. The name Peter means rock. I have Doug make a low mound of earth near the driveway under the big maple, and ask him to set the rock upright on it. The rock

JULY 1996

PETER'S ROCK

becomes a memorial to Peter, and I plant the mound with moss and ferns.

Next, I begin the task of finding enough earth to turn the sloping land behind the boulders into a terrace. I get two yards of soil from a friend, and then a third, but soon realize this job is too big for me. I contact Bill Williams, the man who cuts my lawn; he looks after everything, and in a few weeks I have my terrace. I plant three junipers where the grass meets the boulders, and add Mugho Pines and Winter Heather on the downhill side. When those two conifers grow a bit, they will make a nice foreground to the house. Things are taking shape. The next time Anne comes to see me, we place some of Peter's ashes under his memorial rock. And when Heather next comes to visit, she finds a beautiful and distinctive stone on a beach to place at the base of the big rock. When morning sunlight slants through the big maple's branches, Peter's Rock gleams. Each day that I drive past it, I remember my brother—my best buddy.

Chapter 10

Winter-wild Weather

BLOWDOWN ON DRIVEWAY

Winter is when the community opens up to itself. The summer residents return home and so do the tourists, the resorts close their doors, bed-and-breakfast owners take a holiday, friends and relatives no longer come to visit, and boats are put into storage.

Quadra has its share of winter weather—storms, snow, frost, fog—and rain. Southeasterly winds unleash their wild fury to race across the island. Those who live on Quadra's south and east coasts, particularly on the waterfront, often watch in awe as waves sweep in with tremendous power. Huge logs, tree stumps and other debris crash and crunch against the rocks and/or each other with a fearsome noise, heightened by the sounds of wind and stormy sea.

Sea gulls, like tumbling acrobats, frolic with the wind, testing their flight skills: they veer sharply to one side, then swiftly turn to rise up before dropping back down. Expressing their exuberance in a series of aerial manoeuvres, they call out in high-pitched exultation. On shore, the tops of the tall conifers that edge the beach lurch back and forth and side to side like drunkards, waving their black silhouettes against storm clouds and the dark distant mountains. The thrashing sound of the trees joins with the crashing waves, the banging logs and the squealing gulls in a cacophony of sound that spells "storm."

Because my house is in the lee of a hillside, I am protected to some degree from the vicious southeasterlies, but not entirely. In a windstorm, torn branches come flying down with enormous force, and the broken pointed end of a maple or alder branch can bury itself quite deeply in the ground.

After one windstorm, I get in the car to head for the ferry with fifteen minutes to spare. As I curve around the driveway, I come face to face with a large hemlock that has fallen and lies diagonally across my path. The trunk itself, I notice, is high enough off the ground to allow me to pass underneath, so I run back to the house, grab the pruning shears, and clip open an archway through the down-hanging branches. The car just squeezes through, and I manage to catch the ferry. Later, I find that two other trees are down in my woods, and have them bucked, split and stacked in the woodshed for firewood for next winter, when they will have dried out.

Another winter when a southeasterly is blowing, I have a 1 P.M. appointment with a group of volunteers to collate the pages of the island's monthly publication, *The Discovery Passage*. I slip on a warm jacket and outdoor shoes, then go down four steps into the hallway. Just as I put my hand on the front doorknob, a clear voice inside my head says "Bathroom." So I turn around, kick off my shoes (it's an island habit), and walk to the bathroom.

Once there, I realize I have absolutely no need to use the bathroom and wonder why the command was so strong. Oh well, now that I am here, may as well make use of it. A few moments later, I hear a loud FWUMPH outside. Something has succumbed to the windstorm. I return to the hall, put on my shoes again, and get in the car.

I head down the driveway, make the curve—then brake to a stop. Ahead, lying right across the driveway, is half of a tall, double-trunked maple tree. One of the trunks has split away at the crotch, where rot often occurs, and has partially buried itself from the impact of the fall. The branches spread out at least 6 m (20 feet).

I sit at the wheel, frozen with shock. I realize that going to the bathroom took about the same time it would have taken me to fasten my seatbelt, back out of the carport, turn the car around and go down the drive. I would have been hit by the falling tree. The wind is howling in fury. Shaken, I decide not to travel tree-lined roads in such a wind; there will be enough volunteers to do the work anyway. As I back up, I realize that Peter's memorial stone is to one side of where the maple has fallen . . . Thank you, Peter.

When the lights flicker, it is usually a sign that the power is about to go. But I always have matches and candles ready as well as a coal-oil lamp, and my cast-iron wood stove will ensure continued warmth; also, I can cook on its flat top. There is no knowing how long the power will be out. It can be hours—or days.

It's not only the wind, snow or bad weather that can cut off the power. On three occasions when I was without electricity in good spring weather, I checked with a neighbour and found the outage to be quite local. A phone call to the hydro company brought a truck and servicemen over on the ferry. The first thing they did was check at the base of my power pole, and often there was the culprit, a dead crow. Crows, it seems, have a habit of standing on the transformer at the top of the pole. With one foot on a live wire and the other on something grounded, they form a short circuit. With a pfft and a flash, several homes lose power. This seems to happen mostly in the spring when a lot of young crows are about, a hydro man tells me.

One evening in early March, I am about to head for bed when I notice my deck is all white. SNOW. It's a hand-span deep, and inwardly I groan. Suddenly, a brilliant white flash lights up the whole property, accompanied by a TZZT sound, and the house is plunged into darkness and silence. I get out an extra quilt and go to bed. By morning, a really deep snow has reshaped the world into a soft white roundness. The indoor temperature has dropped to 55°C (about 13°F). Without showering (the water isn't hot enough), I don my thermal gear, a jacket and a woollen hat. After lighting the wood stove, I eat a bowl of cereal, fill the bird feeders, and carry in a large supply of wood. Once the stove heats up, I make coffee, toast and poach an egg. The silence is eerie: no hum of the fridge or the ceiling fan, no click of the electric baseboard heaters turning on and off. Worst of all, no CBC radio. The phone is out too. I feel isolated, marooned.

I can hear the crack of treetops and branches breaking under the weight of snow. Later, I walk around outside; it's hard going in such deep snow. The driveway is littered with broken branches; three tall alder trees and two hemlocks are down. Nature is thinning and pruning her own.

After lunch, I'm startled to hear a knock on the door. It's Tanya Storr, a young reporter/writer from up the road. "I'm going to walk to the Cove," she says. "Can I get your mail for you?" "Yes, please," is my answer. She tells me that last night the hydro transformer blew and the area affected by the blackout is extensive. At dusk, I light the coal-oil lamp and three bright red candles left over from Christmas, then settle down to handwrite long letters that I never could find the time to write, until now.

I am not a winter person and I don't enjoy snow. I much prefer a green world to a white one. Snow is cold, wet, messy and hangs around too long. And deep snow can be very hard on the deer and the birds. For the deer, I cut cedar boughs from the roadsides and stick them upright in the snow for them to eat. For the birds, I hang suet in addition to filling the bird feeders hanging from the carport rafters and scatter seed on the snow. From dawn to dusk, the carport is aflutter with dozens of Juncos flitting and fighting, coming and going and chasing each other. The year-round Towhees make room for several Varied Thrushes: one time I count six. Fox Sparrows and

POTTERY BIRDFEEDER

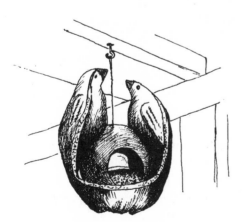

COCO-NUT BIRD FEEDER

VARIED THRUSH

BIRDS FEEDING IN DEEP SNOW

Red-shafted Flickers politely wait their turn, but then down come the Steller's Jays. Squawking, blue wings flapping, these greedy "make-room-for-me" birds scare off most of the others. I watch all this from a kitchen window so I can check on when more seed is needed. When the snow is thick on the ground, the big dish needs replenishing three times a day.

Like the birds, I long for the meltdown when I can see everything green again, when I don't have to park my car down by the road to ensure I can get out to pick up the mail in the morning. Even then, if road crews have ploughed a fresh fall of snow, I will have to shovel away the wall of snow blocking the entrance to my drive. Unless, of course, my kindly neighbour across the road, Alvin Tye, has got there first.

A storm can be fickle in its choice of who loses power and who doesn't. A few houses or a whole area (occasionally much of the island) can be plunged into darkness. The loss of power usually means a phone call to neighbours to ask: "Have you got power?" The answer can help determine if the outage is local, regional or more widespread, the latter with the potential for an extended time.

In a big storm, friends and neighbours also check on each other's needs and safety by phone—if that's not out too. During one big southeasterly blow, I phone to ask how Joy and Bob are doing. Not well, it so happens. They tell me they recently sold their wood stove, but its replacement, a propane gas heater, has not arrived. Meanwhile, they've been using portable electric heaters, useless now the power is out. To top it off, their car is in Campbell River being serviced. Joy and Bob tell me that they've cooked dinner on the barbecue on the deck, but the house is now getting too cold to stay. With bags packed, they are about to call a taxi to take them to the ferry and a hotel in the River. I insist that they stay with me instead and drive over to pick them up.

As we head back to my place, the wind is still furiously lashing the island. Suddenly, my headlights pick up a large alder sprawled right across the road, from ditch to ditch. It's only minutes since I passed that way. Luckily, it was a dead tree, so it smashed into pieces small enough for us to clear away so we can get the car through. We make it home safely.

·   ·   ·

Since almost all island roads are tree-lined, power and phone lines are always vulnerable to outages for long and short periods. If the power is out, it takes longer to load and unload the ferry because the loading ramp and other equipment have to be operated manually. When a strong southeasterly is blowing, the ferry may stop running altogether. It is not necessarily that the vessel can't make the crossing in safety, but it can't unload vehicles on the Campbell River side, as it is open to southeasterlies, and the wind pounds the upper structure of the vessel, tossing it from side to side like a bobbing cork. This makes it hazardous for vehicles attempting to drive on or off the rocking ferry deck.

The ferry crews, men and women both, are helpful, friendly people, and I know several of them by first name. If loading is slack, we stop and exchange a few words. One time I am driving back from Victoria, hoping to catch the last ferry to Quadra. Outside Campbell River, a slow truck holds me up, and I feel like an impatient hare behind a tortoise, but the road is too winding to overtake. Minutes tick down—too quickly. Will I make it or not? Finally, I turn right into the terminal, thrust my ticket into the hand outstretched from the window of the ticket booth, and race across the empty loading lanes toward the loading ramp and the ferry. Too late. I see the ramp rising up, so I brake to a stop, then sag into my seat like a dropped bean bag. Missed it. But wait. To my astonishment, the ramp stops rising and begins descending to connect with the ferry apron. Metal hits metal with the sound of music as a smiling face and a beckoning hand wave me on board. My return smile and hand-blown kiss send a silent message of appreciation and thanks to a kind-hearted deckhand.

In the winter, I easily get cold feet, so if it's a chilly day and I'm taking the ferry to the River, I go up to the lounge. Choosing a seat by the window, I slip off my shoes and put my feet on the electric baseboard heaters so that by the time I return to the car my feet are toasty warm.

This day I am in the lounge warming my feet, when Elena Mason comes in and we exchange greetings. Taking the seat opposite me, she looks down at the floor and asks, "What's with the shoes?" I tell her that I often slip off my shoes to warm my feet on the heater in winter. Elena continues looking down with a puzzled look and says, "Yeah, but the *shoes*." I don't understand what she means. Equally puzzled, I follow her glance downward to the floor.

To my horror, I see that I have two mismatching shoes. One is a black walking shoe, the other a dark navy low-heeled dressy shoe with a wide instep strap and metal buckle. I laugh and laugh while Elena looks on. When I finish laughing, I explain what has happened. As I was about to get into the car to leave, I realized I had forgotten my list of things to do and to get in town. So I went back inside and kicked off my outdoor shoes. After picking up the list, I returned to the hall but didn't bother to turn on the light this half-dark winter morning. Hastily, I shuffled my feet into two of the four shoes on the floor. Only it wasn't a matching pair.

"What are you going to do," Elena asks, "go home and change?"

"I can't," I say, "my car is on the ferry and we're about to leave."

"Don't worry," says Elena, "nobody will notice."

In the shopping mall, I make a distinct two-toned sound of clunk-umph, clunk-umph, clunk-umph as I walk around, because one shoe has a soft sole and the other a hard one. I feel stupidly self-conscious but at the same time I am giggling inwardly. And Elena is right: nobody notices.

More indelible in my mind than any of these ferry episodes is the time I have to fly from Campbell River to Vancouver for two days of book promotion. My publisher has booked me a return flight from the Campbell River airport, leaving at 5:20 P.M. This means I must take the 4:00 P.M. ferry from Quadra. I drive my car into lane two (our ferry fares are prepaid return, so tickets are only taken on the Campbell River side).

A ferry worker approaches my car in a manner that clearly means he has something to tell me, and I wind down my window. Bending over, he solemnly declares: "The four o'clock on Tuesdays is a dangerous cargo run. No cars allowed." To my horror I realize that this is Tuesday.

Looking around, I notice for the first time that the only vehicles in line are tankers and trucks carrying diesel, propane, gas and such. I had totally forgotten about the dangerous cargo run, as normally I have no need to take a late afternoon ferry. "I have to catch a plane," I blurt out as if my life depends on it.

"No exceptions," he declares and walks away.

Panic wells up. My first media interview is 9 A.M. tomorrow morning, closely followed by others. I'll have to take the water taxi, a large powerful boat that holds twelve passengers. Some of us came back from a New Year's

Eve theatre event by water taxi, and we all shared the one-way fare, which was $70.00 a few years ago.

I pull out of the lineup and race for home and a phone. I have to be on that plane. While I'm fumbling through the phone book, a bright light shines in my head. Eric Peterson. April Point Lodge. I dial the lodge's number, hoping he is not away somewhere or just not around. Eric answers the phone. Before I finish explaining my problem, he cuts in calmly. "Don't worry," he says, "come on down and we'll get you across, no problem." I drive the winding road to the lodge. There, at the side of the wharf is a small boat, engine already running. Smiling, Tony Simard (the lodge manager then) helps me aboard. My panic fades in a warm glow of gratitude.

The sea is glassy calm and white plumped-up clouds are reflected in the grey-blue water, which we skim across like a jet-propelled water beetle. Just as we pull into a marina on the other side, the ferry is docking nearby with its dangerous cargo. I catch the plane.

Bald Eagles are as much a part of Quadra as ravens and deer. For several years, the island has taken part in an annual Bald Eagle count run by the province's Ministry of the Environment, to check on whether these birds are declining or increasing. In addition to British Columbia, the states of Alaska, Washington and Oregon participate in this study, which is always held on a Sunday in January between 10 A.M. and noon. Islander Mary Bennet is the liaison for Quadra, where the count covers mainly the southern part of the island which is accessible by vehicle. She divides this into nineteen areas and, in pairs, participants cover their assigned areas, making note of every eagle they see. They also keep track of whether these are immature or adult birds.

MATURE BALD EAGLE

MATURE BALD EAGLE

MATURE AND IMMATURE BALD EAGLES

This is my first eagle count, and Mary, who lives nearby, invites me to pair up with her. We drive to the end of her waterfront road, binoculars around our necks, and soon spot one mature Bald Eagle perched on a bare branch high in an old fir tree, and an immature just below. The latter are all dark brown for the first two years, then become mottled with white to varying degrees on their wings and breast. It takes five years before the Bald Eagle's characteristic pure white head and tail identify it as a mature bird ready for breeding. The name "Bald" given this eagle seems inappropriate, but in fact it is derived from the word "piebald," referring to its two colours. (It is incorrect to call it a "Bald-headed" Eagle.)

Mary and I drive back down the road and head for the village of Cape Mudge. Thick, dark conifers rise sharply behind the rows of houses, and we scan the forest for any white specks, the quickest way to spot a mature eagle. Soon an immature flies over us, followed by two ravens and a gull. Our count reaches seven, then eight, and we return to the car to drive to the lighthouse, where we walk the shore, looking out to sea and above at the trees. Hearing an eagle's staccato call, we look up to see large, dark wings just above, heading out to sea. Later, an eagle flies parallel to the beach past us, then perches in a tall tree. We walk on and the count rises to thirteen. The next half hour brings it to seventeen.

It is a cold, damp day, and since we've been counting for nearly the required two hours, we decide to head for home. A mature eagle flies across the road, heading out to sea. Then another. We look across to Discovery Passage and see a herring ball; several eagles are already there and others are winging their way towards it, bringing our final total to twenty-four.

Some days later, I hear from Mary that the 1994 count for Quadra Island is 302, well up from the previous year. For the next count, I join my friend Sherry Patterson to cover the April Point area, and this time our total is down somewhat; no herring ball. Several years of eagle counts indicate that these powerful birds are holding their own, neither increasing nor declining. That information, combined with a shortage of government funding, spells the end of the annual Bald Eagle count.

One winter, I decide to make a trail that will wander around my property, touching on various aspects of it. I start with a deer trail that enters the woods from the south meadow and with rake, clippers, shovel and hatchet, clearly define the path, choosing where it should meander. I work on the trail a little each day, and while some days see reasonable progress, some days it takes a lot of hard work to go a short distance. Disused deer trails make for easier going, but often there are fallen tree trunks and large old branches or thick underbrush to deal with.

My trail winds through the woods, passing a bank of young ferns, a large tree stump with springboard notches cut into it from the old logging days, and a hemlock with a bent trunk. The bend probably was formed when another tree fell across its young and pliable trunk, holding it back from straight growth for some years. After emerging from the woods, the trail crosses part of the grass meadow and then plunges back into the forest, dappled in sunlight where ferns and underbrush grow, depending on the amount of light that filters through. It passes the nest of the Winter Wren, now abandoned, then a magnificent old maple, and continues on past a trio of huge tree stumps hardly visible for dead forest debris. After following a wide deer trail, it crosses the driveway, picks up the deer trail again, eventually to meet the other side of the circular driveway. From here, it is back to the house, or alternatively, into the forest on the east side to finally end near the carport.

One morning, when the sun slants into the forest on the west side of the circular driveway, I again look at those three huge tree stumps which stand a short distance from each other. They are hardly noticeable because of the jungle of fallen dead saplings, wind-broken branches and other forest debris around them. These largely concealed stumps are monuments to the kind of forest that once covered Quadra, and I decide they should be a visible reminder of the meaning and magnificence of "old growth." After dragging out all manner of rotted fragments that are leaning against the stumps or piled on top of them, I chop off the lower branches of living trees so that the stumps are visible from the driveway.

Halfway through this task, Al and Irene Whitney arrive for a visit, with their two young daughters Charlotte and Toria. They have returned to Canada for the winter, leaving their ocean-going yacht, the *Darwin Sound* in a safe moorage in Turkey, where they will return to continue voyaging in the spring. The next day, after breakfast, they all offer to help, so I have them clearing debris in the area of the big stump trio. Al swings a mean axe to drop some of the small dead conifers and lower branches, and he takes the opportunity to teach Charlotte how to use one, not a skill much used under sail. Even little Toria makes herself useful carrying armfuls of branches and debris. Irene and I catch up on news while we work. A bit later, we hear Charlotte yelling, "Mommy, Mommy." We both look up. She is running like

FIR TREE STUMP. CIRCUM. 5·4 m. [NEARLY 18']

HEMLOCK GROWING ON OLD STUMP

a yearling across the meadow, ahead of her father, excited and breathless. "Mommy, Mommy, we found some *deer poop*!" I smile, understanding the joy of a new and exciting discovery, no matter what it is.

By the time the Whitneys leave, the three gargantuan tree stumps stand out starkly in dark silhouette against the forest. One is 3.9 m (13 feet) in circumference and the other is 5 m (16 1/2 feet); the two are only 1 m (40 inches) apart. The third has a circumference of 5.4 m (18 feet). As with most trees, conifers grow quickly when they are young and slow down in maturity; the later years add only a little to their girth each year. When these trees were cut down, they must have been three or four hundred years old— though they can live much longer than that.

Mosses and lichens flourish on the rotting bark of many old stumps, particularly the short ones. Seedlings, often hemlock, frequently sprout from the top of a stump, sending long roots down the sides and into the ground.

Sometimes more than one tree grows from the top of a stump. Eventually, when the host stump has become rotted, the tall young tree growing on it may fall in a windstorm, if its roots are inadequately anchored in the ground.

There are several other stumps of great girth in the woods around the property. Standing by the three massive ones, I try to imagine how my few acres must have looked before the first pioneering settlers arrived, when no one but First Nations people made the island their home. I look up, up, up, and imagine those three trees soaring into the sky, reaching probably a height of 70 metres (229 feet) and more, their widespread branches touching each other and leaving little light for the underbrush to grow. I feel dwarfed by the vision of such exuberant growth unimpeded and undisturbed for so long. If only just one of the trio of goliath trees had been left standing, what a monument to the biotic community of Quathiaski Cove it would be. Due to fires and many years of logging on the island, only clusters of large old-growth trees remain, all requiring a hike in to see them, and none remain in the Quathiaski Cove area.

I go from stump to stump, checking them all out. Some have springboard notches on each side, on which the faller stood to cut the tree, using crosscut saws in the old days. I find myself wondering when my property was logged. For the answer, I visit Jeanette Taylor, well known as the island historian. She lives in a house originally built in 1893, now much renovated but in keeping with the period. Huge, raggedy apple trees are a reminder of those early years when farming and self-sufficiency were vital to pioneer life on the island.

Jeanette tells me that the first property bought on Quadra Island (originally called Valdes Island until 1903), was in 1882. Within a couple of years, over 1214 hectares (3,000 acres) were sold or pre-empted. In 1890, Robert Hall, who already owned some land on Quadra, purchased District Lot 134, which included the 1.2 hectares (3 acres) I now own. He had the property logged by Louis Casey, who ran an oxen logging outfit in Quathiaski Cove from 1880 to about 1892. When Robert Hall died, he left his property to his nephew, Dick Hall, who in 1910 sold 194 hectares (480 acres) to Thomas

Noble and family. They were well-to-do British immigrants from England who ran a successful, well-equipped farm, including cows, pigs and poultry. They, too, logged over the years.

Curious to find out when the last of the large trees on my land were logged, I seek out early settler Thomas Noble's grandson, Bruce Noble, who lives in Campbell River. He tells me that through the years logging was done selectively on their extensive Quadra property; smaller trees were taken for pilings, large ones for export or milled for lumber. There was no clear cutting. The last logging took place in the 1950s.

On the vacant land next to mine is a huge log lying close to its 1-m (3 1/2-foot) diameter stump. The end of the log is in good condition, and I count 230 rings, one for each year of its life. I ask Bruce Noble if he knows why there are so many felled logs, some quite large, lying on the ground. He explains that logs with evidence of rot were no good for lumber, and with no pulp and paper industry to take them, they were simply left where they fell.

These felled or windblown trunks, called "nurse logs," lie like raised gardens, covered in moss, lichens, huckleberry bushes, ferns and conifer seedlings. When eventually these logs completely rot into the ground, they will provide nutrients to the earth, nourishing the seedlings they nursed and completing another turn in the cycle of life and death.

Chapter 11

Easy Come, Easy Go

TIGER SWALLOW-TAIL

Standing on the deck, I look around to check out the changes, additions and improvements I have made to

my land over the past few years. The trees I planted, or transplanted, are doing fine; the terrace with the junipers and Mugho Pines looks good, the contoured salal serve as a transition into the forest, and the circular drive adds another dimension to the layout. But it needs a focal point, something bold to catch attention. A gazebo? No, not appropriate. A pond? Nice, but not really a marker. While visiting friends on Denman Island, I discover Michael Dennis's cedar tree sculptures: big, bold, wonderfully creative human figures formed by inverted cedar trunks (culled from logged areas) with appendages added. The one I would like, however, is to be part of an exhibit so is not available. Another is newly finished and Michael is not ready to part with it. We correspond and he sends me photos but purchasing problems remain because he is doing a lot of exhibiting.

One day, I go to the Kwagiulth Museum on Quadra to see a travelling exhibit of photos of Inuit stone monuments. Sizable colour photos show large, vigorous arrangements of boulders, huge ones juxtaposed with others of different sizes and shapes. Some are markers and others have spiritual significance; all are dramatic in their rocky, barren setting against magnificent skies.

I am drawn to these powerful rock arrangements, and they inspire me with an idea for the focal point on my land. I start to hunt for the right boulders. Roy Dahlnas, who is in the excavation business, has some, but they are too rounded and too small. On a hike, I discover some great boulders, but they are not accessible to a road for trucking out. Then I hear about an old narrow road that has been widened and pushed through to a new development area, so I go and check it out. A long, rough, rocky road used by logging trucks leads to the new road and an area where rock has been blasted. To my joy, I see boulders of all sizes, many of them huge. One has a drill hole right through it, another has interesting striations in the rock, and others have attractive facets or one flat side. Not only are they ideal for my purpose, they are right by the road for easy loading. I feel I should get somebody's permission to take them and start by phoning the highways department. No, they don't own them. I check with a real estate agent to find out whose land they are on and phone the owner for permission. "Help yourself," he says laughing.

Back I go to the rocks, with tape measure, masking tape, paper and felt pen. For nearly an hour, I look them all over, considering, choosing, measuring, deciding, changing my mind, re-choosing. The boulders are perfect, and I can't believe my luck. After mentally figuring out how they might go together, I decide on six of varying sizes and put a strip of masking tape on the ones I want, lettering them A to F. Then I draw a rough ground plan of all the boulders, marking the position of those I have chosen, and measure their length and width. I return home, excited at the thought of soon having my lithic monument.

I make a model of the sculpture by cutting styrofoam into pieces that represent each boulder, using my measurements and notes on which side is flat or which has a special feature. My design has two upright boulders and an off-centre crosspiece. Another elongated boulder leans against one of the uprights, and two squarish ones sit on the other side.

I phone Roy Dahlnas about picking up the boulders for me, but he is too busy with major jobs just now. He is the only one on the island with a truck big enough to handle the load, so I phone him from time to time. Still busy. The months go by. Then I too am busy, totally rewriting and updating my very first book about First Nations artifacts of the Northwest Coast. The stone feature slips to the back of my mind, until one day I run into Roy. He tells me that he recently drove past the cluster of boulders I want and that as a result of land clearing, piles of tree roots, stumps and dirt have been dumped on top of them. I am horrified—after all the time I have spent looking for them and working out how to arrange them. "Of course, I can always move the stumps," Roy says.

I get in my car and drive the long, broken rocky road to my boulder cache. Once I get there, I can't believe the mountains of dirt and churned-up forest debris that face me. And it is not just that the boulders are covered; most of them have been bulldozed into a jumble, as though a mighty broom had simply swept them all to one side. It will be impossible to find the boulders I have chosen; upended and tossed around as they are, I won't be able to recognize them. What to do?

I decide to make do with five or six of the boulders which have been left behind in the massive shift. One is quite large, with good facets; one is columnar and another roughly triangular; and there is a fairly small, squarish rock plus a couple of others. The choice isn't as good as the original lot, but the rocks have potential. A few days later, I return with masking tape to number them and map their position. I phone Roy again. Maybe, he tells me, he can do the job in a few weeks when he won't be so busy. He will let me know. Several weeks go by; finally, he phones and we make an appointment. I will meet him at the start of the rocky road and leave my car there (which I am very happy to do) to join him in his truck to drive to the site.

Within minutes of reaching the meeting point, I see a massive truck turning off the highway. It's trailing a flat deck that is transporting the excavator. On the door are the words Roy Dahlnas Excavating. At the wheel is Roy's brother, Leo. A bone-jolting half hour later, we reach the boulder site. I look for the masking tape, but most of it has weathered off. Never mind, I can probably remember which of the boulders I chose. Leo gets out of the truck and walks around the rocks. Pointing to the large one, he declares, "Not *that* one."

My heart sinks. "Yes . . . I'd like that one," I say, glancing at him.

"Don't know if the thumb can reach." Leo unloads the excavator and steers it over to the large boulder. Manoeuvring the steel-fingered bucket to reach beneath the base of the rock, he tries to extend the "thumb" to reach

THE START OF RAVENSTONE

over the top, to grasp it for lifting. Leo tries a few times but just can't make it reach the top edge. More sinking of my heart. Without that big rock, the sculpture is nothing.

Not saying a word, Leo fetches a hefty chain from the back of the truck and wraps it around the big boulder. The excavator's massive fingers and thumb grasp the chain like a string around a parcel, and lift up the boulder. Leo swings it around into the heavy-duty truck, which accepts it with a clunk and a shudder. Five other rocks of varying smaller sizes follow. The excavator is returned to the trailer and secured. In all, it has taken a good hour. At long last, I am within reach of having my monumental sculpture.

I drive home to prepare for Leo's arrival with the boulders, pounding a small stake into the spot where the sculpture is to stand and tying a red plastic ribbon to it. I have spent considerable time deciding where it would look best, picturing it from the driveway, from the deck, from the windows, balancing it with the young trees and the direction of the sun. The chosen place is a rise in the ground, not far from the driveway and near a young conifer.

The huge truck and its trailer thunder up the drive. After being unloaded, the excavator clatters and growls its way over the meadow toward the site. The caterpillar treads churn up the grass and dig in each time the machine swivels to change direction. The damage pains me but it can't be helped. Leo swings the excavator's long arm and lifts out the boulders one by one. Since these aren't the rocks I originally chose, I have no model and no sketch of how the arrangement should be. I am just going to have to figure it out as I go along. First, the big rock. I decide which end is to be up, and which side is to face the house. With the chain still on it, Leo places it right on the red-ribboned stake.

Next, the triangular rock. "Leo, could you take that one and . . . er, balance it on top of the big one?" I ask. "I'd like the narrow end facing over that way," I add, pointing. Skilfully, with studied precision, he lifts and positions the triangular rock over the top of the big boulder, then eases it gently, carefully, down. Perfect.

I scan the other boulders for size and shape, choose one, and decide

"RAVENSTONE". 2m.HIGH [6'7"]

where it should go and which side is up. I do the same with each of the rest, running around from one side of the arrangement to the other, quickly making calculated decisions to ensure the arrangement will look good from all sides. Finally, it is done. All six boulders are in place. Leo drives the excavator back onto the trailer, and I thank him for a job well done.

Once Leo departs, I spend some time replacing the chunks of moss and churned-up turf, stomping them flat. At last, after more than a year, I have my stone creation. I am elated. I admire it from the house and keep returning to the window to enjoy the different way it looks in the changing light as the sun moves across it. I notice that the centre part is reminiscent of a perched raven, so I name the sculpture "Ravenstone."

After dinner, I glance out the window once again to admire the . . . NO! I DON'T BELIEVE IT! The entire stone arrangement is lying flat on the ground, like a collapsed house of cards. I rush outside. The big boulder has tipped over, taking the rock balanced on top with it and knocking over the vertical, freestanding one. I could weep.

Two days later, Leo returns with the excavator. On one side of the big rock is a small hollow in the earth, which made it tip over. He says we need a good-sized rock to fill the hollow and spots just the right one on my snake pit. With powerful arms and strong hands, he picks it up and carries it over to the hollow. I know the big boulder should be partly buried, but I need the full height of it. Leo reassembles the arrangement as before, loads up the excavator and leaves. The caterpillar lugs leave another set of churned-up tracks, and again I spend considerable time repairing the damage. This time, the sculpture stays put.

Perhaps the collapse of the rocks was a playful prank of Raven the Trickster to test my patience.

Several years have passed since I set up the birdbath, and the flat stones that surround the beach-log pedestal have become covered in Beaked Moss, which also grows part way up the log. Both are in the shade and frequently get a wetting from the splashing birds. One morning, I notice that the pottery dish has fallen off the base, but it is not broken. That's odd, because the long nails I drove in around the pedestal's top edge have worked well at preventing raccoons from tipping over the dish. To my dismay, I discover that a woodpecker—obviously a Pileated—has hollowed out the back of the log. A section of the top edge, complete with the long nails, has fallen away, taking the dish with it; a quantity of soft, rotted wood fragments lie piled in a ragged mound. The Pileated has feasted on insects of some kind, leaving not a one for me to identify.

To find a new base for the birdbath, I head for that storehouse of sun-bleached wood, large and small, straight or curved, plain or twisted: the beach. Any beach on the east side of the island is where winter storms and high tides combine to present Quadra with a vast assortment of wood, most of it courtesy of the logging industry.

I drive north up the island until paving gives way to gravel, continuing on until the road peters out at a wide, sweeping bay massed with driftwood ranging in colour from off-white to honey to amber. Some logs have a girth so large that I can scarcely clamber over them. One tree stump has intertwined roots that form a sculpture that would grace any art gallery. Another is a goliath that projects its greatness into the skyline, bold and dramatic.

I try to imagine the power of the waves that tossed these enormous logs and stumps onto the rocks. So high up the beach are some that they will never again return to the sea, to join the ebb and flow of the tides and currents that propel rafts of nomadic wood across the water to other coves, bays and beaches along British Columbia's rumpled coastline.

Searching for a suitable log for the pedestal, I scramble over more storm-thrown logs lying around like gigantic matches spilled from their box. Then, suddenly, there it is. It's the right length, the right diameter, and bleached nearly white. The trouble is, it's too heavy for me to haul over all those beach logs back to the car. I could return tomorrow with a friend to help, but by then it will have floated itself out the same way it floated in.

That's how it is with beachcombing: easy come, easy go. I'll keep on looking. The following week, a visiting friend, Suzie, and I find the ideal log, with attractive knots, and the birdbath is renewed.

RENEWED BIRDBATH

I remember the time I first set foot on Quadra Island, and Bill had said, as we drove off the ferry, "This is Quathiaski Cove." I recall thinking what an odd name it was and that I would never remember it. That same puzzlement resonates in the ears of many people to whom I give my address, especially over the phone. "Er . . . how do you spell that?" I am asked. Often, it takes more than one spelling for listeners to get it right, and sometimes they never do. One time, on the phone to a caller from Ontario, I carefully pronounced Quathiaski Cove. "Oh, come on," she said in a tone of disbelief mixed with amusement.

It's not surprising, then, to receive in the mail a letter with the name Quathiaski misspelled. The first one that I noticed read Quathiaki, which I put down to a typographical error, and the same for Quathisaki and Quathiraski. But when I picked up a letter from the federal government addressed to me at Quathia Ski Cove (does Ottawa think we ski in coves in British Columbia?), and others sent to Quathlashi Cove or Quathkniaska Cove, I began to keep a list of the oddball—and at times unbelievable—distortions of the cove's name.

It is not only the cove's name that gives correspondents trouble, but sometimes the island's name as well. Quadra Island was named for a Spanish explorer who sailed this coast in the eighteenth century: Don Juan Francisco de la Bodega y Quadra. Happily, that was shortened to Quadra; otherwise, correspondents would be in really deep trouble. The island's name also has its distortions: Quatro, Quatra, Quada and Quandra—as well as Quadra Street.

Junk mail adds to my collection of odd addresses, not only misspellings but also duplication: double confusion comes with mail addressed to "Quathiaski Cove, Quathiaski Island" or "Quadra Cove, Quadra Island." From a Seattle art gallery came a letter addressed to me at Quatahiaski Cove, A.K. (I haven't yet figured out the A.K. part). Other cove name variations are Auathiaski, Kuathiaski, Ouathiski, Qualihaski and Waathiasky.

I share my amusement at some of the more far-fetched misspellings with

Nadine Mar, Post Master at the Quathiaski Cove Post Office, which houses our mailboxes. From time to time, when I'm picking up mail or purchasing stamps, Nadine will show me a peculiar address on someone else's mail; it always adds laughter to the rainiest of days. Consider these: Qiatjoaslo, Duathiaflis, Kuaphiasqui, Tuatkisski, Quathlashi, Quatvwasky and Quaphiafiki. And finally, one that takes the prize, for brevity at least: QTSK.

In the first eight years of living on the island, I collect over fifty deviate addresses, and just when I think I must have them all, along comes another, each a bona fide and often brave attempt to spell a somewhat unusual place name. At least it alerts me to the fact that such mail is not from a friend or relative.

Out of curiosity, and for the fun of it, Heather sends me a post card from Old Basing, in England. The entire address consists only of my name and the postal code for Quathiaski Cove. It reaches me in five days, and I show it to Nadine, who hasn't noticed. "I read your name so I just put it in your box," she laughs.

It's a small island.